BIRTHSTONES

Books by WILLARD A. HEAPS

The Bravest Teenage Yanks

The Wall of Shame

Birthstones

BIRTHSTONES

BY WILLARD A. HEAPS

MEREDITH PRESS / New York

Br

Copyright © 1969 by Willard A. Heaps

First edition

Library of Congress Catalog Card Number: 78–75692

MANUFACTURED IN THE UNITED STATES OF AMERICA
FOR MEREDITH PRESS

VAN REES PRESS • NEW YORK

CONTENTS

BIRTHSTONES

CHAPTER 1

THE LORE OF GEMSTONES

The natural history of gemstones is as old as the earth itself. Most of the stones were formed within the earth's crust millions of years ago and the majority are indestructible. Through the operation of various natural phenomena they were developing long before man appeared on the earth.

Man's contact with gems is recent in comparison with the development of the earth. One can only imagine the feelings of the Stone Age man, with his primitive tools, when he first saw the sparkle and glow of gems in their natural state within rocks. Many varieties were not uncovered until recently, but in primeval times those that came to light were given divine characteristics. In the course of time the priest—for beliefs in the unknown creative forces and their relation to man have always had a place in human life, even when they concerned only the observed phenomena of nature—or the ruler of a tribe used the gems to symbolize his divinity and exceptional position.

For this reason, gems were first worn by rulers, who adorned their bodies, costumes, and thrones and furniture with fabulous gems which were mined in their own or other countries. The first known jewelry was

3

worn by an Egyptian queen, Zer, about 5500 B.C., in bracelets of turquoise. The crowns and paraphernalia of the rulers of ancient Egypt and Mesopotamia were of breathtaking loveliness and splendor, adding to the belief that the monarchs were indeed superhuman beings. Royal crowns have always reflected whatever gems were available at the time in their most dazzling forms.

From India and Egypt, Phoenician merchants brought gems to ancient Greece and, later, Rome. Some of these early stones, such as jade, amber, agate, malachite, jasper, and chrysoberyl, have been superseded in popularity by more flashing stones. The "luxury" civilizations declined and disappeared, and the gems of the Middle Ages were of lesser importance in adornment. Only with the growth of the more modern monarchies, with their wealthy noble class, did precious stones again come into favor. The truly fabulous crowns, bracelets, necklaces, and rings worn by royalty and the wealthy since the sixteenth century are more than legends, for many of the stones exist today in museums or on the persons of the extremely rich, the only ones who can afford them. The highly developed craft of the lapidary, or gem cutter, has produced the cutting, shaping, and polishing of precious and semiprecious stones, singly or in combination, of unexcelled beauty.

In order to be classed as a gemstone, a stone must have certain qualities, though few gemstones possess them all. They must be durable, or attractive, or rare. The diamond is durable and beautiful but not rare; the emerald is durable, beautiful, *and* rare. Indeed, the fire emerald is the most valuable stone in the gem world, being rated with the ruby as above the diamond in monetary value.

A concise definition of a gemstone is: a mineral hard enough to take a high degree of polish and durable enough to retain it. Nearly all gemstones are minerals; the major exception is the pearl, which is produced by animal organisms.

The essential quality is durability or hardness, and the gem cutter works to convert a rough rock into a wonderful gem. For purposes of convenience, a German physicist named Mohs at the beginning of the nineteenth century divided mineral hardness into a table of ten degrees, placing diamond, the hardest mineral, at the top of the list with a grade of ten. Talc, the softest mineral, was placed at the bottom of the list with a grade of one. All other mineral substances fall between these two degrees of hardness. Minerals below the grade of five are seldom cut as gems because they are too soft to be durable. Therefore, most of the gems in popular use are between five and nine on the Mohs scale:

10 Diamond
 9 Ruby and sapphire
8½ Alexandrite
 8 Topaz
7½ Aquamarine, emerald, garnet, and zircon
 7 Amethyst, bloodstone, and tourmaline
6½ Opal, peridot, and turquoise
 6 Moonstone
 4 Pearl

Those below seven can easily be carved, and are
therefore used as amulets or charms, seals, and decorative brooches, bracelets, and necklaces. Onyx, which
is used in cameos, agate, lapis lazuli, and jade, none
of them birthstones, are very often carved with decorations of intricate workmanship.

The distinction between precious and semiprecious
gems is entirely one of value and price. The five so-
called precious gems are diamond, emerald, sapphire,
pearl, and ruby. All others are semiprecious. But less
perfect stones and synthetic gems are always currently
available, so one can usually find his natal stone at a
reasonable price.

People have always been attracted to gems, just as
they have to jewelry, the form in which gems can be
best displayed. Few people except collectors would
wish to possess a stone in its natural form, but when
its colors are brought out by masterful cutting, a delicate science, to show its beauty and to bring out its
hidden loveliness, the fascination is readily understood.
A part of this attraction, also, has always been related
to widespread superstitions concerning gems.

An aura of wealth has naturally always surrounded
the wearers of gems. Since royalty and the nobility
were far above the level of the common man, they
could well afford the finest and most costly stones, as
evidences of both power and wealth. The display of
fabulous gems, particularly by ruling monarchs and
women, gave and still gives the wearers an appearance of superiority, as well as presenting specific evidence of their high status. For many centuries, but

particularly in the sixteenth to nineteenth centuries, representatives of reigning monarchs visited far distant lands to procure the most magnificent precious stones of unsurpassed size and perfection. No price was too exorbitant, for funds were apparently limitless.

Even in the present day when few monarchies still survive, the citizens of democracies are impressed and almost overwhelmed by the few collections of crown jewels which are still in existence. The gem collection on exhibit in the Tower of London cannot fail to impress the viewer with the past glories and wealth of the English kings and queens. The Russian crown jewels—at least what remains of them—were cataloged by the Communists after the Revolution and were on public display during 1926; they are now stored in the vaults of the Kremlin. The descriptions and photographs of the pieces in the collection produce some of the sense of awe which must have been the reaction of the serfs of past centuries.

The imperial crown is an example. Ordered for the coronation of Catherine the Great in 1762 but not worn by her because it was not completed in time for the ceremony, it presents an appearance of solidly set diamonds. Indeed, 4,936 diamonds of varied sizes weighing 2,858 carats completely cover the exterior, and the central ridge consists of 37 perfectly matched pearls weighing 763 carats. In the head of the imperial scepter of Catherine was set the fabulous pure-white Orloff diamond of 195 carats which was valued in the inventory at more than a million dollars!

A recent royal display of gemstones, unparalleled

in modern times, was the crown worn by Iran's Empress Farah at her coronation in October, 1967. From the royal jewels kept in the vault of the Central Bank, a world-renowned jeweler chose 1,469 diamonds, 36 rubies, 36 emeralds, and 105 pearls to fashion in six months a crown that is literally priceless. An informal estimate of its value was fifteen million dollars.

Today the symbol of wealth evidenced in jewels is very impressive. Some jewelry is so valuable that the wearer must be accompanied by security guards, and the stones to be worn are removed from safe-deposit boxes or bank vaults and immediately returned to them after being worn.

The cost and value of a precious gem or semiprecious gemstone depend on weight. The unit of measure is the carat; in the international metric system a carat is equal to 200 milligrams and is called the metric carat which is one fifth of a gram or about .007 ounces. To transfer the metric weight to ounces avoirdupois, our system, the number 142 may be used for one ounce. Thus, whenever the number of carats of a particular gem is stated in this book, its weight in more readily comprehended ounces can be easily calculated. Generally the value of a gemstone, per carat, increases rapidly with the weight.

Among women, necklaces lead in popularity, followed by rings, earrings, and brooches or pins. Good taste dictates that a woman should not bedeck herself with too many at one time lest she appear like the show window of a jewelry store. The man of today has less opportunity to wear gemstones, and then only in less showy rings, cuff links, and studs, though in the past men often equaled women in displaying precious stones.

The chief quality to be looked for in a gem is its color; its setting and cut should be designed to bring this out in its most superb loveliness. Many stones are available in a wide variety of shapes. Though not all stones are limited to one principal color, a few of the principal colors are:

Red	Ruby
Yellow and brown	Topaz
Green	Emerald
White and blue	Diamond
Sea-blue (indigo)	Sapphire and Aquamarine
Violet	Amethyst

The colors of nature and the seasons are represented in various gems:

The blue of a placid sea in the aquamarine.
The lovely green of cool grass in the emerald.
The blue of a summer sky in the sapphire.
The glow of a blazing sunset in the ruby.
The soft mellow light of the moon in the moonstone.
The rich warm brown of autumn in the topaz.
A glorious mixture of all the colors of the rainbow
    in the opal.
Nature's finest royal purple in the amethyst.

Lists of birthstones for various months, both ancient and modern, have included stones which represent the spirit and nature of the seasons.

The popularity of certain gems varies according to style and fashion. Such stones as the opal and garnet have enjoyed widespread acceptance at particular times, only to decline with changing tastes and fashion. The five precious stones, however, enjoy continuous appeal, and every woman and girl considers a string of pearls, whether genuine or synthetic, an essential part of her wardrobe, for it can be worn with every costume color.

If financial considerations prevent purchase of one of the five most costly stones, one can still own such a gem, for science has developed specialized techniques to produce synthetic or imitation stones; some of these stones are of such fine quality that they duplicate the beauty of the genuine stone and would be recognized only by a professional jeweler. Though some excellent imitations are made from colored glass, modern chemistry has produced in the laboratory examples which defy detection. Price is the only clue, and this would only be known by the buyer.

In strictly imitation stones, the bright, many-faceted cuts and colors are easily produced by the addition of metallic oxides of various forms to fine glass. For example, iron oxide produces green, brown, and red; copper produces blue and red; cobalt, blue; nickel or manganese, purple or brown; uranium, green or yellow. Other chemicals will produce very clear colors. Since they are molded into shape and therefore do not have to be cut, they will approximate the genuine; hence they are easy and cheap to fashion. Much of what is used in inexpensive costume jewelry is colored glass;

the higher the cost, the more likely it is that the gems will be synthetic.

The term "paste" is applied to all cheap, inferior glass imitations of gemstones. Taken from the Latin word *pasta,* or "dough," a reference to its soft plastic nature, the term was widely used instead of "imitation" before the twentieth century. In the eighteenth century, the making of paste jewelry was a fine art; imitation diamonds, garnets, topazes, emeralds, and rubies were backed with foil to give them greater brilliance. So expert was this work at one time that Madame Pompadour, the power behind the throne of King Louis XV of France, frankly admitted that his favorite gift to her was a lavish necklace of paste diamonds so perfectly executed that no one could tell that it was not genuine. One of the most famous short stories by Guy de Maupassant, "The Necklace," deals with the financial ruin of a minor rank-and-file civil servant whose wife had borrowed from a friend what she thought was a priceless genuine diamond necklace to wear to an official ball. The necklace was lost, and to replace it the civil servant purchased another which was returned to the owner. After ten years of hard luck and penury, it was finally paid for. Only then did his wife discover from her friend that the necklace was paste and worth a mere five hundred francs, not the 36,000 paid for the replacement.

Glass imitations soon lose their brilliance. Impoverished members of the nobility in all countries have often worn excellent paste imitations, however, thus protecting their pride.

BIRTHSTONE LISTS—ANCIENT TO MODERN

MONTH	HEBREWS (BIBLICAL)	ROMANS	ARABIANS	15th TO 20th CENTURY	BRITISH (1937)	AMERICAN (1912)
January	Garnet	Garnet	Garnet	Garnet	Garnet	Garnet
February	Amethyst	Amethyst	Amethyst	Amethyst Hyacinth Pearl	Amethyst	Amethyst
March	Jasper	Bloodstone	Bloodstone	Jasper Bloodstone	Aquamarine Bloodstone	Bloodstone Aquamarine
April	Sapphire	Sapphire	Sapphire	Diamond Sapphire	Diamond	Diamond
May	Chalcedony Carnelian Agate	Agate	Emerald	Emerald Agate	Emerald Chrysoprase	Emerald

Month						
June	Emerald	Emerald	Agate Chalcedony Pearl	Agate Cat's Eye Turquoise	Pearl Moonstone	Pearl Moonstone Alexandrite
July	Onyx	Onyx	Carnelian	Turquoise Onyx	Ruby Carnelian	Ruby
August	Carnelian	Carnelian	Sardonyx	Sardonyx Carnelian Moonstone Topaz	Peridot Sardonyx	Sardonyx Peridot
September	Chrysolite	Sardonyx	Chrysolite	Chrysolite	Sapphire Lapis lazuli	Sapphire
October	Aquamarine Beryl	Aquamarine Beryl	Aquamarine Beryl	Opal	Opal	Opal Tourmaline
November	Topaz	Topaz	Topaz	Topaz Pearl	Topaz	Topaz
December	Ruby	Ruby	Ruby	Ruby Bloodstone	Turquoise	Turquoise Zircon

Imitation pearls of opalescent glass were first produced in France in the seventeenth century. Other "pearls" are ordinary beads covered with a coat of iridescent material.

Substitutes or "look-alikes," called synthetic gems, are entirely different. These are actually made from the same elements of which the genuine stones are formed, combined by chemical processes. Some of these are known by trade names. Quite naturally, the main synthetic stones are those which are the most expensive in genuine form—the diamond, ruby, emerald, and sapphire—though others, such as the zircon, topaz, tourmaline, and Alexandrite, are available. These possess the identical qualities of the real stones. Pigments are added to obtain the correct color or shade. Most are made by heating corundum, or alumina, and adding hydrogen and oxygen. For those whose birthstones are prohibitively expensive, a synthetic stone will prove entirely satisfactory.

The assignment of specific gems as natal stones, according to the month of birth or the sign of the zodiac, goes back to ancient times. The ancient lists include many stones now generally unavailable, and a survey indicates some standardization. In most of the old lists the "warm" or "glitter" stones were selected for the bleak and desolate months and there were many beliefs and superstitions associated with the various stones.

The United States list, "a recognized standard list," was adopted by the American National Retail Jewelers' Association at its 1912 convention. Before that time jewelers used several of the older lists, some of which included stones that were not readily available and were considered out of fashion and unattractive. The gems associated with the signs of the zodiac did not cover the entire chronological months, because the zodiacal signs included parts of two months, ten days in one month and three weeks in the other. The object of the jewelers was to select one gem for each calendar month, with alternate stones for five of the twelve months—March, June, August, October, and December. The adoption of the list was purely for business reasons: a jeweler would be able to recommend the "correct" gem for anyone born during a specific month, without regard for the exact birth date of the purchaser. One who believed in the guidance of astrological signs, however, could—and can still—select the stone covering his birth date according to the zodiac.

In the months before the convention, the subject was thoroughly discussed in the Association's official bulletin, and the convention readily adopted the list submitted, with objections from those few who preferred the zodiacal lists. Some jewelers suggested that the diamond for April should be omitted entirely because of its cost. Others felt that the pearl—June—was not "flashy" and not a true gem, since it is marine rather than mineral in formation.

The British list, adopted by the National Association of Goldsmiths in Great Britain in 1937, was an attempt to correct the duplication of colors in the older lists. It is approximately the same as the American, with an occasional alternate transferred to first place.

Of course, no one needs to observe the listings. Personal preference might lead a person to choose a stone different from one recommended. If the price of the genuine stone is too high, the imitation and synthetic stones may be purchased. Most people prefer to purchase rings, though girls have a wide choice of jewelry set with the appropriate stones, many of which are too delicate and feminine looking to appeal to boys. The latter may purchase large, heavy stones in class, fraternity, and club rings.

Some of the beliefs and attributes in the lore of gemstones may seem foolish to modern young people. Even so, the particular beauty of each birthstone is in itself a source of joy and satisfaction.

CHAPTER 2

THE ORIGINS AND SIGNIFICANCE OF BIRTHSTONES

Precious gems and semiprecious gemstones have been the subject of legends and folk stories since the first recorded stones—the turquoise bracelets of Queen Zer—were worn as ornaments. The strong appeal to the imagination aroused by the colorful, often sparkling, stones was linked with their natural beauty. The blue of the sapphire, the deep red of the ruby, the yellow of the topaz, the green of the emerald, and the rainbow hues of the opal—all were fully appreciated. These products of the earth's inner core were inevitably surrounded by mystery and looked upon with awe, and they soon began to be considered in symbolic ways. The symbolism of colors began to develop and to be related to various phases of life and nature:

White:	Life, joy, and innocence
Red:	Divine power, love, fire, and human emotions
Blue:	Heaven, virtue, and truth
Green:	Hope, faith, and victory
Purple:	Suffering and sorrow—still recognized as the funeral color along with black, the color of mourning
Yellow:	God's goodness and faith

These colors are still used symbolically in the vestments of the Church.

The first association of a special gem with each month was probably suggested by the original breastplate of the High Priest of the Hebrews made by Moses about 1250 B.C. according to instructions he received during his forty days in the mountains, as recorded in Exodus 28. These included specifications for the materials, size, and arrangement of twelve gems in four rows. The gems were to represent the twelve tribes of Israel, and the names were to be engraved on the stones. The breastplate was to be worn by the High Priest, Moses' brother Aaron.

Exodus 39:8-21 again describes the gems used:

>First row: sardius, topaz, carbuncle
>Second row: emerald, sapphire, diamond
>Third row: ligure, agate, amethyst
>Fourth row: beryl, onyx, jasper

The ancient names used were later translated into modern equivalents by Flavius Josephus (A.D. 37–95) who was then the High Priest:

>First row: sardonyx, topaz, garnet
>Second row: no change
>Third row: amber, a variety of agate, amethyst
>Fourth row: aquamarine, onyx, jasper

These identifications were also made by Pliny, the first natural scientist, who wrote a 37-volume History of the World, the last volume being devoted to gems, which he described as to physical properties, occurrence, and the love of the stones as then known. Most of our knowledge of gems in Roman times has been obtained from Pliny's work.

Interestingly enough, almost the same twelve stones are recorded in Revelation 21:19-21, the final book of the New Testament, as the stones in the foundations of the wall of the Heavenly Jerusalem.

The twelve gems in the breastplate were later linked with the twelve signs of the zodiac and came eventually to be associated with the months of the year, each month having a specified stone as its own. A natal gem was supposed to possess occult powers and peculiar virtues and evils which would exercise a lifetime influence on the person born during the particular month to which it was assigned. Every phase of life—health, love, daily activities, wealth, and happiness or unhappiness—was believed to be influenced by the natal stone.

The ancients believed that from the knowledge of the location of each planet in the heavens at the exact date and hour of his birth a person could foresee what kind of a life he would have. In astrology, a belt in the heavens, called the zodiac, was divided into twelve sections, called signs, of about thirty days each. These signs were said to determine the characteristics of the individual and the influences on his life. Today they appear as horoscopes—daily, monthly, and annual—in which astrologers try to foretell the events of a person's life and warn of coming events.

These signs of the zodiac, with gems assigned to them, were worked out long before the Roman calendar was devised. The astrological division of the year was

based on the equinoxes—the time when the sun crosses
the equator and the day and nights are everywhere
of equal length—these being approximately March 21
and September 23. The heavens were mapped out with
constellations symbolized by mythological figures and
animals; those in the belt along which the sun made its
yearly course were called the zodiac. The zodiac forms
a circle of 360 degrees. However, there are 365 days
in the calendar year—366 in a leap year which occurs
every fourth year—so the signs do not change on the
same date every year, but will vary with each year.
The dates in the chapter headings of this book follow
the course of one particular year. From earliest times
these signs were engraved or used as jewelry designs
for persons born in the different zodiacal periods.

The table for the twelve periods of the year in ancient
times determined the gems which were appropriate:

SIGN	APPROXIMATE—DATES	GEM
Aries	March 21–April 19	Diamond
Taurus	April 20–May 20	Emerald
Gemini	May 21–June 20	Pearl, Moonstone, or Alexandrite
Cancer	June 21–July 22	Ruby
Leo	July 23–August 22	Sardonyx or Peridot
Virgo	August 23–September 22	Sapphire
Libra	September 23–October 22	Opal or Tourmaline
Scorpio	October 23–November 21	Topaz
Sagittarius	November 22–December 21	Turquoise or Zircon
Capricorn	December 22–January 19	Garnet

Aquarius	January 20–February 18	Amethyst
Pisces	February 19–March 20	Aquamarine
		or Bloodstone

Throughout the centuries, astrologists have established systems involving the correlation of the zodiac signs with the gods of ancient mythology and their related minerals. For example, Mars, the Roman god of war, was associated with the strong red of the ruby, signifying command and the fire of warfare. However, such relationships are very complicated and since they form an involved area in astrology, they are not treated at length in this book.

When the American National Retail Jewelers' Association compiled its standard 1912 list based on the calendar months, some objections were raised to the differences between the zodiacal and calendar month. Adapting each birthstone to a calendar month was perhaps a simplified method, but it was not astrologically accurate, for an astrologist cannot reconcile any list giving months since he believes the zodiacal division of the year to be correct.

The longest period of the zodiac sign at the beginning of the month was therefore used for that entire month. For example, the garnet as the birthstone for Capricorn, December 22 to January 19, became the gem for the calendar month of January. Those who follow the signs of the zodiac as given in horoscopes continue to consider each gemstone as applying to them only if their birth date is included in the sign. For that reason, successive chapter headings by month include the assigned zodiac period.

At first, people wished to own all twelve principal stones, wearing a different one for each month, but later each person wore the stone of the month in which he was born.

Each month had a precious or semiprecious gem assigned to it and a birthstone superstition grew up that conformed in general to the characteristics of an individual born under the specific zodiac sign.

The following is a general summary for the major stones:

January	Garnet	Constancy and fidelity
February	Amethyst	Preventive against violent passions
March	Bloodstone	Steadfast affection, courage, and wisdom
April	Diamond	Purity, repentance, and innocence
May	Emerald	Discovers false friends and insures true love
June	Pearl	Wealth
July	Ruby	Insures forgetfulness or cure of any ills arising from love or friendship
August	Sardonyx	Married happiness
September	Sapphire	Frees from enchantment; denotes repentance
October	Opal	Misfortune and hope
November	Topaz	Fidelity and friendship
December	Turquoise	Great success and happiness; prosperity in love

A few variations occur in this rhymed version of the mystic lore of birthstones from an unknown source:

Let JANUARY's maiden be
All GARNET gemmed with CONSTANCY.

In fitful FEBRUARY it's a verity
The AMETHYST denotes SINCERITY.

But oh, what shall a MARCH maid do?
Wear a BLOODSTONE and be FIRM and TRUE.

The APRIL girl has a brave defense
The DIAMOND guards her INNOCENCE.

Sweet child of MAY you'll taste the caress
Of EMERALD's promised HAPPINESS.

PEARLS for the girls of JUNE the precious wealth,
And to crown it all they bring her HEALTH.

The RUBY stole a spark from heaven above,
To bring the JULY maiden fervent LOVE.

The AUGUST maiden with sweet simplicity
Wears SARDONYX, gem of FELICITY.

Out of the depths shall SAPPHIRES come
Bringing SEPTEMBER's child WISDOM.

OCTOBER's child in darkness oft may grope,
The iridescent OPAL bids it HOPE.

Born in NOVEMBER happy is she,
Whom the TOPAZ teaches FIDELITY.

DECEMBER's child shall live to bless
The TURQUOISE that insures SUCCESS.

Dreams about gems are said to reveal the influence of the stars and planets, regardless of the dreamer's assigned birthstone. Many "dream books" have been

written or compiled since ancient times, and every object seen in a dream is given a special meaning. The
following list compiled by George F. Kunz, a modern
American authority on gem superstitions, suggests their
significance:

Amethyst	Freedom from harm
Aquamarine	New friends
Bloodstone	Distressing news
Diamond	Victory over enemies
Emerald	Much to look forward to
Garnet	The solution of a mystery
Moonstone	Impending danger
Opal	Great possessions
Pearl	Faithful friends
Ruby	Unexpected guests
Sapphire	Escape from danger
Sardonyx	Love of friends
Topaz	No harm to come
Tourmaline	An accident
Turquoise	Prosperity
Zircon	A heavy storm

Another ancient gem classification is planetary. In
a Chaldean list, for example, stones were attributed to
the seven planets and associated with their related
colors. Various lists differ in their allocations, but a
general classification used by ancient astrologers included the following:

Topaz	gold	Sun
Pearl	silver	Moon
Ruby	red	Mars
Sapphire	blue	Jupiter

Diamond	black variety	Saturn
Emerald	green	Venus
Amethyst	purple	Mercury

In their attempts to control the beliefs of their followers, some ancient astrologers even designated certain talismanic gems as appropriate to be worn on a specific day of the week:

Sunday	Pearl
Monday	Emerald
Tuesday	Topaz
Wednesday	Turquoise
Thursday	Sapphire
Friday	Ruby
Saturday	Amethyst

The astrologers fail to state whether this classification replaces the monthly gem or is in addition to it. Certainly only a person of considerable wealth would be able to afford to possess such a collection!

The traditional designations for wedding anniversaries go back many years in social usage. The standard list, which includes each year for the first fifteen and each five years thereafter, was intended as a guide to the products which were considered proper to present to the married pair as gifts. The suggestions for the first fifteen years can be obtained in inexpensive form; for example, the first was paper, the second cotton, the fifth wood, and the tenth aluminum (originally tin). Starting with the twentieth—china—more costly items are listed, and after the twenty-fifth—silver—gems were assigned.

These are:

30th	Pearl
35th	Coral—not a gem
40th	Ruby
45th	Sapphire
50th	Gold—not a gem
55th	Emerald
60th	Diamond

These gems are the most costly, and undoubtedly only a family member close to the couple would give such a present. In actual practice, it is the husband who traditionally gives the wife a ring, necklace, bracelet, brooch, or pair of earrings containing the gem to celebrate the anniversary. Some objections have been made to the placing of the diamond at the end of the list, for such a gift would probably not be enjoyed for many years and would therefore be passed on as an heirloom. A young wife who had not received an expensive diamond at her wedding would undoubtedly welcome the anniversary gift of a finer one when she would have more of her lifetime to enjoy it. Hence the diamond is being given more and more to celebrate the silver anniversary.

Much of the lore linked with birthstones, which goes back to ancient times and was particularly strong during the Middle Ages, is considered absurd today. One need not accept these superstitions in any way, yet they are fascinating, if only to suggest the great, often consuming, interest the stones have aroused.

CHAPTER 3

GARNET

JANUARY—CAPRICORN (December 22—January 19)

Mention of this name today is apt to create three reactions: The garnet is red, it is so common as to be undistinguished, and it is cheap. The first two preconceptions are incorrect. Few semiprecious stones are found in as wide a variety of colors. And although garnets are readily available and inexpensive, they may still be cut to make a fine impression. In fact, some of the most beautiful crystal forms cannot be distinguished from their inexpensive rivals of the same color. Garnets have a long and honorable history, but for some reason, perhaps the introduction of more dazzling synthetic gems, they have varied in fashionable acceptance. Laying aside these prejudices and misconceptions, a January-born individual can always find a stone to her or his liking.

Garnets exist in all colors and hues and are found in all parts of the world. The garnet is not a single mineral but a group or family of stones with the same chemical composition but different properties. All are silicates, but the various metal elements such as manganese, iron, calcium, and chrome make them different. Each of these combinations results in a particular color and each has its own scientific name: pyrope, ruby red;

almandine, gold-red to violet; spessartite, brown; de-
mantoid or andradite, greens from emerald to olive;
and grossularite, yellowish-red to cinnamon. These are
rarely found in the same place.

The name garnet comes from the Latin *granum*,
"grain," or *granatus*, "seed," because the majority are
very tiny and, of course, worthless as gems. Small
pebblelike garnets are found in abundance in streams
or sandy accumulations. The largest stones are imbedded in rocks, but they have little usefulness as they
are mixed with other substances. A massive ten-pound
stone measuring more than six inches in diameter was
uncovered in 1885 in New York City, during excava-
tions on West 35th Street, a short distance from Macy's
store!

Though the red Bohemian garnets—pyropes—are
still the best-known, almost every color and color combination may be found in different localities throughout
the world—green in the Ural Mountains of Russia, inap-
propriately named the Ural Emerald, as well as in
South Africa, where it is called South African Jade;
brownish-green, or "gooseberry", in Siberia; rose-red
and purple in North Carolina; brownish or orange-red
in Bavaria, the Tyrol, Brazil, Ceylon, Virginia, and
Nevada; violet-red in India, Ceylon, and Malagasy;
and orange-red in Ceylon. Red stones like the Bohemian garnets of Czechoslovakia are also found in South
Africa, where they are called the Cape Ruby. Garnets
of many colors are found in more than a hundred
places in the United States.

The first garnet mines were opened in northern Bo-

hemia, now part of Czechoslovakia, in 1771 and flourished for a century and a half. The gems, originally
locked within the rocks in the mountains, loosened as
the rocks weathered and spread through fluvial deposits
under layers of soil or clay where they are worked even
today, though on a less vast scale than formerly. When
the Bohemian garnets, ranging in reds from brownish-
red to crimson color, were at the peak of their popularity
in Victorian England, more than ten thousand workers
were employed—three thousand of them as cutters—
and these finest of all garnets were exported to every
part of the world. They are still used in necklaces,
brooches, bar pins, pendants, earrings, beads, cuff links,
and scarf pins and, unless set in platinum with other
stones, are within the price range of almost anyone.
Jewelry in designs of all kinds is produced by a Czech
government cooperative, and the garnet is the national
gem of Czechoslovakia.

The small seedlike garnets are widely used for industrial purposes. They are of importance as a jewel in the
bearings of watches and scientific instruments. Most
garnets used in this way are chips produced during the
cutting of gem garnets in Czechoslovakia and Malagasy.
Well over 250,000 are used monthly in the movements of inexpensive watches. The fine Swiss watches
use only the ruby and sapphire for this purpose. In the
United States, garnet is mined for use as an abrasive,
either as garnet sandpaper, which is produced mainly
in northern New York state, or as a loose-grain powder
for grinding and polishing plate glass.

With their twelve-sided crystals, garnets are excellent

for use as small stones in jewelry, and by special cutting can be given a beautiful fire. Inferior stones, however, become dark and lose some of their brilliancy. The general impression is one of warmth and charm. Previous prejudices that perhaps got started because garnets were worn in quantity as old-fashioned parures—matched sets of earrings, necklace, and brooch—and chokers, are disappearing.

The most famous garnet collection is in the Museum of Bohemian Garnets at Trebenice in northern Czechoslovakia, where the best stones produced throughout the years are to be seen in a glorious panorama of red. A stone once owned by King Rudolf II of Bohemia is the size of a pigeon's egg. The most impressive jewelry is a matched set of bracelets, rings, earrings, and a five-strand necklace of dark-red garnets, a family heirloom owned by Verike von Lewetzow, whom the German dramatist Goethe loved in vain.

Another prize Bohemian garnet, weighing 468 carats —over three ounces—and once owned by the King of Saxony, is now in the Dresden Museum. The Vienna Museum possesses a red stone as large as a hen's egg. But garnets need not be so large and impressive in order to be beautiful.

Like other gems many superstitions are attached to them. In these the wearer is promised many good things, so many that even a firm believer in the power of gems might well question the effectiveness of the garnet.

The tradition of this stone began far in the past. The

Talmud states that Noah's Ark was illuminated by a finely cut stone. Snakes and serpents were also said to have been guided by a garnet light in the forehead or mouth. The garnet was the fourth stone in Aaron's breastplate, and the fourth heaven of the Koran was built of garnet. Ancient warriors believed that it was an aid to victory, and the Crusaders wore it as a protection against wounds and accidents in their travels.

Asiatic soldiers used garnets as bullets, in the belief that their glowing color might cause them to inflict a more deadly wound. The gemmologist Frederick Pough reports that in 1892, during a native rebellion in India, Hanza tribesmen fired at British soldiers using garnets as bullets.

In medieval days garnets were supposed to possess curative powers. In addition to protecting the wearer against the effects of poisons of all kinds, they were said to cure depression and offer protection against bad dreams. The red varieties relieved fever; the yellow gems were prescribed for the treatment of jaundice.

In more modern times these gems, among other benefits, have been said to endow the wearer with a light heart, loyalty, and unchanging affections. The garnet is also regarded as encouraging success in business, adding to its owner's reputation, and increasing his popularity.

But throughout its long history, the garnet's main quality has been to insure constancy:

> The gleaming garnet holds within its sway
> Faith, constancy and truth for one away.

And a young maiden wearing this gem was possessed
of admirable and welcome qualities:

> By her who this month is born,
> No gems save garnets should be worn;
> They will insure her constancy,
> True friendship and fidelity.

CHAPTER 4

AMETHYST

The beautiful variations from violet to deep purple make February's natal stone one of great beauty. As more and more sources are discovered, this once costly semiprecious stone has become relatively inexpensive, and since most of the qualities traditionally associated with it are positive rather than evil, it might be called a happy stone.

The word amethyst comes from the Greek *amethystos* meaning "without drunkenness" or "not drunk," literally unable to become intoxicated. The story of the stone's origin is told in a myth. Bacchus, the god of wine in classical mythology, was offended by Diana the huntress. Determined on revenge, he declared that the first person he met as he went through the forest would be eaten by his tigers. As it happened, the first person to cross his path was the beautiful maiden Amethyst on her way to worship at the shrine of Diana. In terror, she called upon the goddess to save her, and before his eyes Bacchus observed the maiden changed to a pure white, sparkling image of stone. Realizing his guilt and repenting of his cruelty, Bacchus poured grape wine over her, thus giving the stone the exquisite violet hue of the amethyst. The carryover to nonintoxication was quite logical, and in ancient Rome amethyst cups were used for wine so that the drinker would have no fear of overindulgence.

Amethyst is a variety of quartz, the most common of all the minerals found in the earth's crust. In the world of birthstones quartz supplies more different varieties than any other mineral in crystalline form. The amethyst is transparent, but bloodstone (March), sardonyx (August) and opal (October) are crypto-crystalline (quartz with hidden crystals which make them opaque). The six-sided crystals of the amethyst are generally imbedded in matrix—mother-rock—or found in pebble form in river gravels. They are very clear.

The colors vary from the palest violet to the deepest purple, with many intermediate shades like bluish vio-let and reddish purple. The deeper the color, the less brilliant is the stone. Gemmologists have assumed that the color is caused by manganese, but this has never been proved.

The principal contemporary sources are Brazil and its neighboring country Uruguay, where the finest gems are mined. These have superseded Siberian reddish-purple stones from the Ural Mountains which once outclassed all others in richness of color. For many years these classic amethysts were mined by political convicts who had been sentenced by the Russian im-perial government, but the mines have been long aban-doned by the Communist regime. Gems currently mined in Brazil and Uruguay are often incorrectly called Siberian amethysts. Other major sources are

Ceylon and New Zealand. Maine, North Carolina, and Pennsylvania are the principal sources in the United States.

The amethyst has enjoyed a long history of social acceptance and has appeared on the majority of historical birthstone lists. It was well known in ancient times, and we read that Cleopatra's favorite among her fabulous jewels was an amethyst signet ring with the engraved figure of Mithra, the principal Persian god in the fifth century B.C.

The religious associations of the stone continue to this day. Amethyst was the ninth gem, the third stone in the third row, in the High Priest's breastplate. In the Roman Catholic church it is still called the Bishop's stone and is worn by the highest ranks of the clergy. This tradition was carried over into the Church of England and the Episcopal Church in the United States, but the ruby and sapphire have also been used. The Bishop's ring with a very large, perfectly cut amethyst has been the symbol of ecclesiastical dignity since the sixth century and is generally worn on the second finger of the right hand.

The papal ring set with an amethyst was first worn in the thirteenth century. Conferred upon the Pope at his investiture, it has the official name of "the ring of the fisherman" because it is engraved with the figure of Saint Peter casting a net into the sea from a boat. A solemn ceremony, which began in the sixteenth century and is still observed today, requires the breaking of the amethyst in front of a conclave of cardinals after a

Pope's death. A new ring is then prepared before the
election of the next Pope, with a space for his name left
blank. When the new Pope has chosen his name, the
ring is engraved with it.

Another of the amethyst's honors is as a stone of
royalty. Throughout history monarchs and members
of royal families have always considered the amethyst
as representing power and the particular prerogatives
of monarchs; hence the terms "royal purple" and "born
to the purple." In England the first monarch to wear
the amethyst as a royal emblem was Edward the Confessor, the last of the early Anglo-Saxon kings, in the
early eleventh century. His crown contained eleven
other gems and was used in coronation ceremonies
until the time of Queen Elizabeth I. The meaning of
the amethyst was stated as follows: "The purple putteth
the King to discharge his duty and legal function sith
that (so that) he challengeth the wearing of purple
robes."

The glowing beauty and attractive color variations
and varying sizes, shapes, and prices contribute to the
amethyst's continuing popularity. It is used in rings,
pins, clips, necklaces, and earrings, and, unlike many
other gems, blends well with gold, silver, and platinum
in settings. The color variations of the amethyst are
also effective with stones of contrasting colors. The best
amethyst is considered to be the deep purple of perfect
transparency, with uniform hue throughout—in other
words, a flawless stone.

The amethyst's history has been long and impressive.

The early Egyptians believed it possessed a power for good, and the tombs of the pharaohs always contain specimens. It ranked among the precious stones of the Bible and was one of the gems used in the foundations of the New Jerusalem. In early Arabian mythology the amethyst was supposed to protect its wearer from gout and bad dreams.

As has been noted, the Greeks originated the name. In addition to the prevention of intoxication, its magic power was extended to cover protection from all harm. Roman wives cherished it above all gems because of the belief that it would preserve the continuous affection of their husbands.

During the Middle Ages, when pseudoscientists and soothsayers were playing upon the superstitions of the people and preparing elixirs from cracked or bruised stones as medicines for both the soul and the body, to the amethyst was attributed the power of keeping one wide awake, sharpening the wits, and protecting its wearers from sorcery. This was one of the several gems which gave victory in battle.

In addition to its religious significance, the amethyst was the stone of Saint Valentine, whose day is still observed in February. He was said to have worn an amethyst engraved with the figure of Cupid, his assistant.

Since purple, together with black, is the color of sorrow, the gem has also taken on that symbolism.

In all ages the amethyst has represented sincerity and contentment. Other particular beliefs have been numerous. It was thought to bring protection from the fury of the elements. One ancient belief held that if the name of the sun or moon was engraved upon it and the stone hung about the neck by the hair of a baboon or the feathers of a swallow, its wearer would be safe from hailstorms!

Romance received considerable assistance. The amethyst would make one's love life smooth and bring lasting happiness to lovers. Continuous peace of mind and contentment were also assured:

> The February born will find
> Sincerity and peace of mind.

This was expressed in another way:

> Let her an amethyst but cherish well,
> And strife and care can never in her dwell.

Were it not for the unchallenged supremacy of the four precious stones, the amethyst might become one of the preferred gemstones. Even so, it ranks in popularity and acceptance with them. Its natural beauty and unique color make the February-born fortunate in being able to wear this regal gem.

CHAPTER 5

AQUAMARINE OR BLOODSTONE
MARCH—PISCES (*February 19–March 20*)

AQUAMARINE

Called the "poor man's diamond," the bluish variety of the aquamarine is one of the most attractive and least costly of the semiprecious stones. The name was first used by the Romans: *aqua*, meaning "water," and *mare*, "sea," because it was so like seawater that it became invisible in it. According to an old myth, aquamarines were originally washed ashore from the depths of the sea where they had lain in the jewel caskets of sirens.

The aquamarine is a member of the beryl family—the mineral beryllium. It is thus a near relative of the deep-green emerald. It appears as free, six-sided crystals in rock veins which have been unaffected by the shock and weathering which destroys many gem deposits. On the Mohs scale of hardness the aquamarine is exceeded only by the diamond, sapphire, ruby, Alexandrite, and topaz. The best cuts possess a transparency and brilliance equal to its sister gem, the emerald. No satisfactory synthetic stone has yet been produced.

The color varies from deep blue to blue with green in different intensities. The deep-blue shade, of which the best specimens are found in Brazil, is rare and therefore most expensive. Value depends upon the depth and shading of color, as well as freedom from flaws. An aquamarine, of course, is not as expensive as an emerald or ruby, but the fine stones are durable and have good wearing qualities.

The stone is found in every continent, but in addition to Brazil, the best stones are from other South American countries, especially Colombia, from the Ural Mountains of Russia, the island of Malagasy, and India. Rocks in many places in the United States yield gems of good quality but not in the preferred deep shades; Colorado, Maine, and North Carolina are the best American sources.

Aquamarines were not popular in our country until about 1906, when Vice President William Howard Taft gave President Theodore Roosevelt's daughter Alice— of "Alice-blue-gown" fame because she invariably wore that shade of blue—a beautiful heart-shaped stone. Aquamarines immediately became fashionable and much in demand, a good example of the way in which some lesser-known gems attain popularity. In the 1930's the Brazilian government presented a large stone of rare quality to President Franklin D. Roosevelt, and Mrs. Roosevelt gave her new daughter-in-law a beautiful pendant necklace as a wedding present.

Fine examples are to be found in most museum gem collections or exhibits. These are often of immense size and indicate the large number of gems which can be cut from a single boulder. The largest aquamarine stone in the world, weighing fifty-six pounds, about 25,000 carats, was on display by the Brazilian government in

New York in 1946; it was eleven inches high and ten inches in diameter. A large stone weighing two hundred pounds was exhibited in Berlin, Germany, before World War II, after which it was broken up into 200,000 carats, or one hundred pounds, of the finest gems. The British Museum possesses an excellent stone weighing almost half a pound, and one of the finest-cut aquamarines is a dark-blue stone weighing 187 carats which is in the Smithsonian Institution.

Though well-known and revered, the aquamarine was rare in ancient times, and first came into prominence among the Romans who considered it sacred to Neptune, the god of the sea.   ▪

Beginning in the Roman period, the stone was regarded as having medical and healing powers. What may have been the first eyeglass in history was a large and perfectly formed gem used by the Emperor Nero over two thousand years ago. Though it was long thought to be an emerald, evidence indicates that it was an aquamarine, which would be more appropriate since it would be clearer. The question, however, is still unsettled. Much later, aquamarines were used as glasses in Germany to correct short-sightedness, and the German name for eyeglasses today is *Brille*, derived from the mineral beryl.

The Romans also believed that the aquamarine could cure ailments of the stomach, liver, jaws, and throat. This view was held during the Middle Ages, when it was also considered effective as an antidote against poison. In an English poem written in the fourteenth century, *The Vision of Piers Plowman,* the wearer of an aquamarine is said to be miraculously protected from poisoning.

Another superstition in the Middle Ages attributed the power of soothsayers to the aquamarine. It was called the "magic mirror," and its use in telling fortunes and answering questions about the future was specifically described in manuscripts. Fortune bowls marked with the letters of the alphabet along the edges were filled with water, and a ring set with an aquamarine was held in the water suspended by a thread. When questions were asked, the ring was supposed to spell out the answers by going from letter to letter just as the pointer in a modern Ouija board spells out the words. There was apparently no end to the gem's psychic and mystical powers.

The aquamarine has always been considered the sailor's gem, promising prosperous and safe voyages and protection against the perils and monsters of the sea.

More recently other powers have been attributed to this gem. For example, a wearer will become quick-witted. For lovers who marry it will aid in increasing and guarding their affection.

Few gemstones have such a firm place in tradition, legend, and history. Apart from its mythical, magical qualities, the blue of the aquamarine is indeed one of the masterpieces of nature.

BLOODSTONE

The alternate March natal stone takes it name from

the belief that it was first formed at the Crucifixion of Christ. When a Roman soldier-guard thrust his spear into His side, drops of blood fell on some pieces of dark-green jasper lying at the foot of the cross, and since that time these stones with particles of red in them have been known as bloodstones.

The ancient name was heliotrope, which is still preferred in England. The word comes from *helios,* the Greek word for "sun," and *tropos,* meaning "change." Pliny wrote: "If placed in a vessel of water and exposed to the full light of the sun, it changes to a reflected color like that of blood. Out of water, too, it reflects the figure of the sun like a mirror, and discovers the eclipse of that luminary by showing the moon passing over its disk [the eclipse]."

Bloodstone is a form of quartz, a variety of chalcedony composed of a compact opaque mass of many intergrown crystals. It is unique among mineral stones in that its color and form is always the same—dark green, spotted or mottled with red. The only variation is in the number and size of the red flecks.

In its natural form bloodstone is found imbedded in rocks and as pebbles in riverbeds. Pieces weighing as much as fifty pounds have been discovered in India where the best quality and greatest size are located. Brazil and Australia also produce good specimens.

When cut and polished, bloodstone has a hard, waxy appearance, and it has been a favorite material for carving religious subjects, presenting a challenge to the craftsman to bring out the effective contrasts. The subject of most of these carvings is, of course, the Crucifixion. One of the most famous, done by the Italian Matteo del Nassaro about 1525, is "The Descent from the Cross." It is in relief, with the natural red spots showing the wounds of Christ and His drops of blood. The Louvre in Paris has a very fine cameo of bloodstone which depicts the scourging of Christ, the red spots representing blood on His garments.

Bloodstone is always cut in rounded form with a flat surface. The Babylonians made many seals and amulets of the stone, which was also a favorite of Roman gladiators. Today it is used mainly in signet rings carved with crests and monograms. Because of its simple form, it is especially appropriate for wear by boys and men who find the more flashy cut stones inappropriate and gaudy.

Because of the religious significance of the Crucifixion, the bloodstone has always been regarded with awe and superstition. According to Pough, prophets playing upon the superstitions of the people and their lack of curiosity about scientific fact, extended the magic of this stone further, claiming that it had actual power over the sun itself and could cause storms and tempests. By waiting until bad weather approached, they claimed to bring on storms, and then professed to interpret future events as revealed to them by the howling winds.

During the Middle Ages, the bloodstone was said to possess curative powers, particularly in stopping nosebleeds. A 1483 book told of its value for this, and an early English doctor called it "the special stone to staunch blooding and good against poison." Powdered and mixed with honey and white of egg, it was supposed to be a cure for tumors as well as stopping all types of hemorrhage. It was also used to draw out the poison of snakes.

A Renaissance belief held that the wearer of a bloodstone could be made invisible. In the *Inferno,* Dante, speaking of the damned on the way to eternal darkness, cited the heliotrope:

> No hope had they of crevice where to hide,
> Or heliotrope to charm them out of view.

And in the *Decameron,* Boccaccio stated, "The other stone is heliotrope, which renders those who have it invisible."

According to other beliefs, the bloodstone could calm the wrath of kings and despots, would enable its owner to open any door, "burst bonds asunder," and would make cold water boil if dropped into it.

In more modern times, the bloodstone has been said to give courage to the wearer and sustain bravery in the face of danger as well as giving him wisdom, particularly in detecting the plots of enemies.

According to an old rhyme:

> Who in this world of ours their eyes
> In March first open shall be wise;
> In days of peril firm and brave,
> And wear a bloodstone to their grave.

Those born in March have an interesting choice of natal stones. A woman can wear the sparkling aquamarine, and men will probably prefer the bloodstone, which is more masculine and subdued in comparison.

CHAPTER 6

DIAMOND

APRIL—ARIES (March 21–April 19)

Diamond! No other word in the realm of gems arouses as much interest. No other stone, precious or semiprecious, holds such fascination for everyone, from the mineralogist and gem specialist to the ordinary person, even a person who can never hope to possess one of whatever size. No other gem makes the pulse beat faster, triggering the imagination and conjuring fabulous stories of wealth, romance, and adventure. No other gem has been the object of more intrigue, greed, and crime throughout history. No other stone has aroused more envy toward its possessor or pride in its owner. And quite possibly diamonds have brought more bad luck to their owners than any other stone.

A diamond is one of the most precious of all gemstones and the most desired. It has been called the king of gems; the gem above all other gems, the master of them all; the loveliest product of nature; and the most powerful stone with the greatest influence in human affairs. Its very name is linked with the Greek word *adamas* meaning literally "invincible" or "unconquerable," and with the Latin words *adamare*, "to fall in love," and *adamas*, meaning "hard" or "invincible." The English word diamond derives from the Middle

English *diamant,* which is identical in French. The diamond is indeed invincible because it is the hardest substance known, natural or artificial. This quality accounts for the fact that it was unknown in ancient times, since its beauty does not become apparent until it is polished and "worked." Only comparatively recently has its brilliance and wonderful play of light been realized. In addition to its decorative beauty, with which we are concerned, it is also invaluable for industrial uses.

In its natural form the diamond is pure carbon crystallized in cubes; it therefore consists of the same material as the graphite in a pencil or the purest coal. It possesses a magic brilliance called diamantine luster, and of all gems it has the greatest refraction and dispersion of light. This accounts for its well-known play of colors and its fire, or flashes of brilliant light. For that reason it is sometimes called "ice," a term used by thieves in the underworld.

Diamonds exist in many colors from white to brown —and even black. Most used as gems are colorless and transparent, but different shades of yellow and brown, or straw color, are common. One of the most unusual of rare diamonds is the Tiffany, a deep, almost orange, yellow. Light, apple-green stones are much less common, and blue is rare. Red is the rarest, and only small crystals have been found; a fair-sized ruby-red diamond among the Russian crown jewels is an exception. The colored stones are generally pale.

Diamonds were first discovered in India, perhaps around the year 1000. The Indian monopoly was destroyed when finds were made in Brazil in 1725. However, the event which brought this gem to world attention occurred in 1867 when some children playing on a farm in the Orange Free State of the Union of South Africa picked up a stone which proved to be a colorless diamond weighing 22½ carats. This set off a diamond rush similar to the United States' gold rush of the mid-nineteenth century, and the African diamond industry still thrives and enjoys a virtual world monopoly. Huge stones continue to be found, the latest—the seventh largest in the world—in May, 1967, in the new African kingdom of Lesotho. It weighed 601 carats and when cut up will undoubtedly yield over a million dollars' worth of stones.

Deposits have been discovered in several other localities in Africa, and in Australia, Borneo, and in central Siberia in 1954.

Diamonds are thought to have been formed first some sixty million years ago. In their natural state they are found deep in the earth in volcanic rocks which have undergone enormous pressure and temperature changes. They also appear in stream gravels in the form of small grains and pebbles. The early South African diamonds were found in river diggings and gravel deposits. Soon after they were mined by simply digging farther and farther into the earth's surface, leaving huge open holes like craters. Today, mining is almost all underground.

The splitting of large stones, called cleaving, is a crucial and nerve-racking process, for should a cleaver strike the stone in the wrong place a diamond worth many thousands of dollars may be ruined. After cleaving, the pieces are sawed to different sizes and cleaned and polished before cutting is undertaken. These methods are the key to a diamond's beauty, and diamonds may be cut in many shapes. The less expensive, very small diamonds called chips are fragments from this cutting process.

Diamond production and supply are strictly controlled by De Beers Consolidated Mines, Ltd., of South Africa which produces 98 percent of the world's diamonds today, so that prices can be maintained at an even level. The demand is continuous.

The synthetic stones which have been produced are not yet suitable as gemstones, but because of their hardness are invaluable in industry, particularly for drills and for cutting the hardest of steel. Imitation diamonds backed with foil are used extensively in costume jewelry.

The most famous diamonds have been mined within a comparatively recent period. Their immensity and fabulous beauty are such that volumes have been written about them and their histories, making highly interesting, though often sad, reading.

The world's largest diamond is the Cullinan, found in 1905 in Transvaal, South Africa, and presented to King Edward VII on his birthday in 1907. It weighed 3,106 carats, or slightly over twenty-one pounds, in the rough, but was cut into two large stones: Cullinan I, now called the Star of Africa, 530 carats, the biggest cut diamond in the world; and Cullinan II, 317 carats. In addition, 103 other stones, nine large and ninety-six small, were cut from this large diamond. Number I is in the royal scepter of England, number II is set in the royal crown. These diamonds are part of the English crown jewels and are on display in the Tower of London.

Second in size is the Excelsior, found in South Africa in 1893; it was 995 carats in the rough and was cut into twenty-one stones. The Great Mogul, the largest diamond from India, where it was found in the seventeenth century, weighed 787 carats in the rough. It has completely disappeared.

Next in size is the Jonker, found in Pretoria, South Africa, in 1934. It weighed 726 carats uncut, and produced 371 carats in twelve beautiful stones.

The Vargas from Brazil, found in 1938, weighed 726 carats and was cut into twenty-nine stones. The Jubilee from South Africa was found in 1895, weighed 650 carats, and was reduced to 245 carats when cut.

The Orloff, which formed the top of the Russian royal scepter, weighed 195 carats. It is said to have been stolen from a temple in Mysore, India, where it was one of the eyes of an idol. This is one of the few million-dollar diamonds still in existence.

The Regent, or Pitt, diamond—410 carats in the rough, 137 carats cut—was found in India in 1701. Its violent history included the murder of the original owner, the sailor-thief who sold it to Thomas Pitt, the English governor of Madras, who in turn sold it to the Duke of Orleans, regent of the French king, Louis XV. It became a part of the French crown, but was stolen during the French Revolution, after which it disappeared and was finally recovered. Napoleon had it mounted in the hilt of the sword which he carried when he was crowned Emperor of France in 1804. It is now displayed in the Louvre.

The largest diamond on exhibition in the United States and the thirteenth largest in the world is the Portuguese from Brazil. Weighing 127 carats, it has a bluish cast and is in the collection of the Smithsonian Institution.

Further along in the list there appears the 106-carat Koh-i-Noor, "Mountain of Light", stone, probably the best-known of all diamonds. It was owned by an Indian rajah in the fourteenth century and presented to Queen Victoria in 1850. It may be seen with the English crown jewels in the Tower of London.

The stone best known to Americans and certainly one of the prime bearers of bad luck to its owner is the 44½ carat Hope diamond, which is of an outstanding blue color. It was thought to have been made from a larger stone called the Tavernier Blue which was stolen from the royal French collection in 1790 but reappeared mysteriously in the London gem market some forty years later as a smaller stone and was purchased by Sir Henry Hope, a British banker. Later it was sold to the Sultan of Turkey, then to Mrs. Evalyn Walsh McLean of Washington, to whom it brought nothing but unhappiness. Valued at over two million dollars in 1962, it is now in the Smithsonian Institution.

The list could be expanded indefinitely. However, no account of diamonds can omit the tragic and involved story of the French Queen Marie Antoinette and of a diamond necklace which was a factor in her being guillotined during the French Revolution, even though she never saw or touched the necklace. This necklace consisted of 647 diamonds, the greatest gem masterpiece in all history. It had been ordered by King Louis XV for his mistress, Madame Du Barry, but the monarch died before it was completed. For nearly ten years the jewelers tried to sell it to his successor, King Louis XVI, and his wife, the extravagant Marie Antoinette, but neither would buy it because the price was too high.

A sinister and cunning plot to steal the piece was devised by the Countess de La Motte who persuaded Cardinal de Rohan, at that time out of favor in the French court, to believe that the Queen wished to purchase the necklace secretly. The Cardinal arranged for the purchase and without having paid for it he handed the necklace over to the Countess, who promptly took it to England where it was broken up and the diamonds sold separately. The scandal and trial that followed the disappearance of the notorious jewelry rocked the throne of France, and the whole affair, which took place in 1786, was one of the factors in turning the populace against the monarchs, eventually leading to the French Revolution.

The tales of diamonds are seemingly endless, but one relating to their hardness is particularly interesting. Queen Elizabeth I was noted for the number of her devoted admirers during her long reign. One of these was Sir Walter Raleigh, who spread his cloak in the mud so that the Queen could walk on it. He once wrote with the diamond of his ring on a windowpane. "Fain would I rise but I fear to fall." Later, when he had fallen out of favor, Elizabeth used her own ring to write below his inscription, "If thy heart fail thee, do not rise at all."

The diamond has always been the gem in engagement rings, and the smallest ring in history was put on the finger of two-year-old Princess Mary Tudor, daughter of Henry VIII, by Cardinal Wolsey when she was betrothed in 1518 to the baby Dauphin of France. This was one of the youngest engagements in recorded history.

The lore of diamonds is closely associated with the development of refinements of cutting methods. Until the fifteenth century it was less attractive, and tales dealt with rough rather than finished stones. When its hardness was conquered, the diamond triumphed.

In the High Priest's breastplate the sixth stone, said to be a sapphire because of its colored transparency, was probably a diamond. Moses was said to have used it to cut the rocks for the Tables of the Law as well as for fashioning the breastplate.

Oriental lore is filled with mentions of the diamond. The Hindus believed that it was formed by lightning striking rocks. Some of them, noting that the stones were often found after heavy rains that washed away the clay hiding them, believed that they grew. One of the tales of Sindbad the Sailor in the Arabian Nights told of an unapproachable valley the ground of which was studded with loose crystals. Pieces of meat thrown from the surrounding cliffs were picked up by eagles who carried the adhering crystals to their nests from which they were gathered by brave and terrified explorers.

Many of the older myths and even more modern tales dealt with the diamond's hardness and shape in uncut form. There was a belief that a diamond would break the teeth if put in the mouth or rupture the intestine if swallowed. A flawed gem was believed to bring misfortune, and the shape of an uncut stone, according to Pough, was considered significant. A triangular stone was believed to cause quarrels, a four-sided stone to cause terrors and fears, and a five-sided stone to bring death. Only a six-sided stone was lucky. Swallowing of diamond dust was supposed to be fatal.

A widely held belief first mentioned in the Talmud was that the diamond was dark or brilliant according to the guilt or innocence of the wearer. To a five-pointed stone now owned by the Shah of Iran has been attributed the power of making conspirators confess their crimes in the Shah's presence. Mary, Queen of Scots, was given a diamond as a talisman against danger and poison.

The Greeks, who gave the diamond its ancient name *adamas*, firmly believed that fire and water had no effect upon it. It was able to overcome poisons, end delirium, and banish needless worry. It curbed violent feelings and thoughts of murder, lessening anger and strengthening love. The diamond was also an unfailing test for fidelity, because, it was said, a stone placed on the breast of a sleeping loved one caused the sleeper to tell the most intimate of his or her secrets. If it was placed on a wife's head without her knowledge, she would, if faithful to her husband, turn to him in her sleep; if she was false to him she would move apart.

In medieval times its powers resembled that of several other gems. Like them, it was a valuable charm against plague and sorcery and aided its wearer in performing heroic deeds.

More modern beliefs involve good luck and happiness. The wearer is given strength of both character and body and is able to resist temptation. Its greatest power is to give purity, innocence, and virtue to the wearer; this explains its use as an engagement gift, a pledge to the betrothed.

> She who from April dates her years,
> Diamonds should wear, lest bitter tears
> For vain repentance flow, this stone,
> Emblem of innocence is known.

The diamond is the national gem of England, the Netherlands, and, quite appropriately, South Africa.

CHAPTER 7

EMERALD
MAY—TAURUS (April 20–May 20)

This placid gem of spring, one of the four precious stones, is possibly the most beguiling of all gems. It is truly the stone of nature, its restful green suggesting natural scenes. Pliny, the Roman authority on gems, believed that the emerald "out-greened" nature itself. "No other color," he wrote, "is so pleasing to the sight; for grass and green foliage we view indeed with pleasure, but emeralds with so much greater delight inasmuch as nothing in creation compared with them equals the intensity of their green. Besides, they are the only gems that fill the eye with their view, yet do not fatigue it." And in the eleventh century an abbot writing in Latin verse, said,

> Of all green things which bounteous earth supplies
> Nothing in greenness with the emerald vies.

The green of the emerald varies from rich velvet or satiny to grass-green or blue-green. Ireland, because its lush foliage most nearly approximates the true emerald green, is called the Emerald Isle. The deepest shades are the rarest and most expensive when they are almost flawless. A nearly perfect stone is literally beyond price, and all fine specimens command one to five times the price of the finest diamonds of equal size. Small stones may cost from one hundred to several hundred dollars a carat, while large gems may reach a thousand dollars and up per carat. Almost all emeralds, even the finest, contain flaws, for they are not found perfectly developed in nature.

Emerald is one of two varieties of the mineral beryl which are natal stones, the other being the aquamarine of March. It is a silicate mixed with aluminum, varying from transparent to translucent. The green color is thought to be due to the presence of chromium. The crystals are six-sided and of regular shape. Because of its brittleness, the emerald is not easily carved except by experts. Emeralds are made brilliant only by expert cutting. The name comes from the Persian word *zummurrud* meaning "green."

The history of the emerald and its availability goes back far into antiquity. Well-known in Babylon and Egypt, emeralds were then owned and worn regularly by royalty. Mines in southern Egypt near the Red Sea were the source of Queen Cleopatra's famous stones, which she preferred along with pearls. They have been found on Egyptian mummies buried centuries before Christ.

The emerald was well known in Biblical times. It was the third stone in the High Priest's breastplate, and the prophet Ezekiel said of tribal merchants, "they traded their wares with emeralds." The fourth foundation wall of the New Jerusalem was made of emeralds.

From Egypt emeralds were sent to Rome, where

they became a symbol of wealth because of their rarity. As already noted, Nero's eyeglass was thought to be a grass-green emerald, but it more probably was an aquamarine, which is clearer.

But the emerald's importance really began when Marco Polo brought some back to Europe from his famed long-distance travels during the last two decades of the thirteenth century; and three centuries later the fame of the emerald was further enhanced by fabulous stones sent back to Spain from Mexico, Peru, and present-day Colombia by the Conquistadores. The temples and graves of the Incas, who considered the emerald as representative of the green earth and therefore a sacred stone, were systematically pillaged; even though the natives were tortured in order to make them tell the locations of the mines, they were never revealed.

Colombia, north of Peru, is today the source of the most perfect emeralds to be found anywhere in the world. They are mined from formations of limestone, particularly at Muzo, near Bogotá, an Inca mine discovered in 1558 by the Conquistadores. Other contemporary sources are the Ural Mountains of Russia, Norway, Austria, India, Malagasy, and Australia. The only source in the United States is North Carolina, and the gems found there are of small size.

Excellent synthetic and imitation emeralds are on the market, and these are almost impossible to distinguish by the naked eye. Though German chemists attempted to reproduce the lovely green of the emerald, the process of slow crystallization was discovered by an American scientist named Chatham in 1935, and the best synthetic stones bear his name. Imitation emeralds are made of colored cut glass; they are welcomed because of their low cost and are widely used in costume jewelry.

Famous emeralds are quite numerous and are proudly displayed by museums and private owners. The Holy Grail Cup has belonged to the Cathedral in Genoa, Italy, for over seven hundred years. It was supposed to have been "borrowed" from King Herod's banquet table by the Disciples for use by Jesus at the Last Supper, and it was brought to Genoa by Crusaders returning from the Holy Land in the twelfth century.

The King Alfred Cup is now in an Oxford museum, to which it was given after its discovery in 1693. The Saxon king was known to have used it in 858. It is oval shaped and is decorated with semiprecious stones. Around the side in letters of gold run the words "Alfred ordered me to be made" in Gaelic.

The most fabulous use of emeralds was in the Crown of the Andes, which was set with 453 emeralds weighing 1,523 carats, over ten ounces. The center stone was forty-five carats. The crown was said to have been worn by the last Inca king of Peru when he was taken prisoner by the Conquistador Pizzaro in 1532. It was sold to an American syndicate in the 1940's and is now broken up. These stones are probably being worn today by wealthy American women.

The largest known emerald, now in the British Museum, was owned by the Duke of Devonshire and is

called the Devonshire Emerald. It was presented to
one of the Duke's ancestors by Dom Pedro when he
was Emperor of Brazil between 1824 and 1831. Nearly
two inches in diameter and slightly more than ten
inches long, the stone weighs nearly ten ounces, or 1,384
carats.

The Vienna Museum has on display a jar nearly five
inches high which was cut from a two-thousand-carat
emerald.

The French royal jewels, which included many emeralds given by Napoleon to Josephine, were sold, but
the Russian Czars' collection is with the Kremlin crown
jewels. It includes an emerald of thirty carats which is
considered the finest cut emerald in the world.

No greater edifice of strange beliefs ever surrounded
a gem than that built around the emerald. Most of
these promised happiness rather than unhappiness.

According to Hebrew tradition, a serpent that fixed
its eyes upon an emerald became blind. The Persians
believed that the stone gave security to the wearer;
around a richly carved seventy-eight-carat stone was
engraved the inscription, "He who possesses this
charm shall enjoy the special protection of God." It
would also give peace of mind. The stone's healing
powers were not overlooked. Lapidaries, or gem crafts-
men, could rest their eyes from their fatiguing work by
gazing from time to time on an emerald. The Persians
also believed that it was valuable for curing liver and
stomach complaints.

In the Middle Ages a wearer would be given the gift

of prophecy; to secure its aid in foretelling the future, the stone was to be placed beneath the tongue, or if the alphabet was arranged around a bowl and an emerald suspended in it, a message regarding the future would be spelled out. Furthermore, a liar would give himself away when an emerald was shown to him. Wise men emphasized its power to protect the chastity of women. Its medical uses were numerous; an emerald would sweat in the presence of poison in the body. The water in which an emerald had been soaked was used to bathe inflamed eyes, and the stones were ground—the pharmacists do not say how this hard stone could be pounded to dust—into a fine powder and placed in the eyes for treatment of infection.

Later on, during the Renaissance, lovers could use the changes in the gem as a test for fidelity:

> If faithful, it is like the leaves of spring;
> If faithless, like those leaves when withering.

Royalty and the nobility gave an emerald to a loyal friend, with the reminder that the gem would not break so long as faith and friendship remained firm.

In all periods the emerald has been the symbol of serenity and peace of mind. This may have been a reflection of the ability of things green to calm the human spirit. Along with this came freedom from any evil and the restoration of peace when troubled.

Happiness and contentment were to be the wearer's reward:

Who first beholds the light of day
In Spring's sweet flowery month of May
And wears an emerald all her life,
Shall be a loved and happy wife.

The emerald is the national gem of both Peru and Spain.

CHAPTER 8

PEARL, MOONSTONE, OR ALEXANDRITE
JUNE—GEMINI (May 21–June 20)

PEARL

The appearance of the pearl on a gem list might at first seem odd since the pearl is not a mineral, but, like amber and coral, is a so-called organic gem. Nevertheless pearls are among the most sought after and valuable gems and compete with diamonds as the most popular and most constantly in fashion. Tradition has included them in all books on gemology, for they are worthy partners of precious and semiprecious stones. Pearls are also unique in that they are often cultivated rather than found in their natural state. The pearl is the only gem which does not have to be cut and polished; it has its own luster and is ready to use in jewelry when it is taken from the shell in which it has grown.

Pearls are found in oysters and clams and are chemically composed of forms of calcium. The shells of the pearl-growing varieties of these shellfish are very hard, and have a thick layer of iridescent mother-of-pearl which is used for cameos, buttons, knife handles, and other decorations. It is wishful thinking to hope to find a pearl in an edible oyster, for only rarely are they found in them, and even then they are far too tiny and too lusterless to be of value.

The formation of pearl has been likened to human cancer. If a very small foreign body such as a sand grain, a parasite, or a fragment of rock finds its way into the shell, irritation is set up. The oyster then begins to cover the irritating matter with layers of shell material exactly like the outer shell covering. Layer after layer is formed, like the layers of an onion. As a result of such an accident, the jewel we know as pearl is created.

There are several types. Blister pearls are formed when the irritant grows on the inside of the outer shell and must be cut away; they are of little value and are used in the cheapest forms of pearl jewelry. True pearls form in the tissues and are generally spherical or pear-shaped; these are the most valuable. Very small pearls are called seed pearls.

Cultured pearls are formed by the human introduction of tiny particles of mother-of-pearl into the fleshy part of oysters. They look as real as natural pearls, and after this method was discovered in 1912 the term "cultured" was agreed upon rather than "artificial" or "imitation." The imitation pearl is made by enclosing a glass bead in layers of iridescent liquid; when these coatings are dry, the appearance is similar to the genuine. Imitation pearls are used in less expensive costume jewelry.

Size and shape are two determinants of value. The size varies with the size and strength of the irritant rather than that of the oyster and will vary from very large to the smallest seed pearls. Their weight is gauged not by carats but by grains; a grain is one fourth of a carat. The majority are round, but some are pear-shaped; and these are used as pendants in necklaces and earrings. Others are oval or egg-shaped.

Color and luster are also important. There are many varieties. Color depends on the locality in which they are found. In the Persian Gulf and Ceylon the pearl found is creamy, called Oriental, though some have a rose-pink tinge and others possess a slightly yellow hue, as do those from the West Indies. Black pearls, richly prized, are found chiefly in the Gulf of Mexico and in the waters near some Pacific islands. But clear white is the best as well as the usual color. Their luster, the reflection of light from them, should be iridescent; this is caused by water temperature. Jewelers have great difficulty in matching pearls for a perfect necklace because each pearl must be nearly identical in size and luster.

Natural pearls are found throughout the world in warm salt water. Divers bring up baskets of oysters and clams which are then opened for the removal of the pearl, but only about one shell in a thousand contains a pearl. Some freshwater pearls have been found. Cultured pearls are specially bred, mainly in Japanese waters, in huge oyster beds; young two-or three-year-old mature oysters are injected with the irritant and returned to the water in mesh baskets, regularly fed, and finally, after as long as seven to nine years, harvested.

The pearl is a feminine gem and, whether genuine or imitation, it is prized since the jewelry can be worn with any color. Rings are least desirable because pearls are round and their extreme softness—two on the hardness scale—makes them easily injured. Genuine pearls retain their natural form and sheen for a much longer period than cultured pearls; the average life is about a century and a half, though some have kept their beauty for many centuries. Their beauty and comparative rarity are always appreciated, for a fine pearl is said to be the most perfect natural gem. The appearance of fine pearls improves if they are worn constantly, for if not used their luster is dimmed. In ancient times people believed that pearls were alive and were nourished by the skin of the wearer; if neglected they lost their luster and were said to have "sickened." Cultured pearls tend to become discolored and should therefore be cleaned regularly and, if in necklaces, must be restrung.

Because of their unique beauty in the finest natural form, famous pearls have been both notable and numerous.

Experts consider the most beautiful of all pearls to be La Peregrina (The Wanderer), so-called because of its history. Found in Panama four hundred years ago by a Negro slave who was said to have been given his freedom in exchange for it, the pearl was sent to King Philip II of Spain by his conquistadores in 1570. This matchless pearl is white, pear-shaped, about 1½ inches long, and weighs 111 pearl grains, equal to over 27 carats. It hangs from a diamond-studded platinum mount. From Spain it passed successively to Mary I ("Bloody Mary") of England and Prince Louis Napoleon of France. When he was short of funds he sold it to the British Marquis of Abercorn; then it disappeared for a century. Early in 1969 La Peregrina turned up at a New York auction house, and the successful bidder was actor Richard Burton, who purchased it as a birthday gift for his actress wife, Elizabeth Taylor. La Peregrina has often been confused with another one of the Spanish crown jewels, a perfectly round pearl called La Pelegrina, sometimes spelled Pellegrina.

The so-called Pearl of Asia, given by the Indian Shah Jaehan to his favorite wife, for whom he built the Taj Mahal, is the largest in the world, the size of a pear; it is three inches long and nearly two inches across and weighs about a third of a pound. The Shah of Iran owns a pear-shaped pearl of approximately the same size which is valued at about $320,000.

The most famous pearl necklace was that given to Catherine de' Medici by Pope Clement when she married the future Henry II of France. It consisted of six long ropes of thirty-seven large teardrops threaded on gold wire. Catherine gave them to Mary, Queen of Scots, as a wedding present in 1559, and after that tragic lady was executed, Queen Elizabeth I purchased them. King James I then inherited them and gave them to his daughter when she became Queen of Bohemia. Returned to the English royal family, they became known as the Hanoverian pearls.

Pearls have always been a sign of wealth, and have often been preferred to the four precious gems. They were frequently used as medicine, for they could be easily crushed because of their softness. The most famous story of the drinking of pearls concerned Queen Cleopatra of Egypt and a banquet she prepared for

Mark Antony. When he expressed his astonishment at its lavishness, Cleopatra removed one of her pear-shaped eardrops, dissolved it in vinegar and drank to his health, saying, "My draught to Antony shall far exceed it." A similar act was performed by Sir Thomas Gresham, who was the financial agent of Queen Elizabeth I. When she visited the Foreign Exchange, he pledged her health in a cup of wine in which a pearl worth fifteen thousand pounds, an enormous sum, had been crushed.

The love of pearls dates back to ancient times, but the superstitions concerning them are not as numerous as those for other gems. However, their romantic and poetic associations are greater. The first jewel mentioned in the earliest decipherable and translated writings of ancient Egypt was this lustrous beauty. Pearls are also frequently mentioned in the Bible, Talmud, and Koran.

Arabians called them the "tears of the gods" since they were supposedly formed by drops of rain falling into open oyster shells. Warriors of India set pearls into the handles of their swords as symbols of the tears and sorrow which the sword might bring. Another belief of the people of India was that during certain months of the year Buddha sent dewdrops down from heaven and the oysters rising to the surface of the water caught and held them until they were changed into precious pearls.

Pearls were first used in medicine in China about 2000 B.C. The Arabs and Persians also used pearls as cures for insanity and various diseases. Cleopatra was not afraid of drinking her dissolved pearl—if the story is true—because it was a custom of the times. However, modern chemists and gemmologists believe only an acid stronger than vinegar would dissolve the powder and that it would be too strong to swallow.

The most long-lived belief was that the pearl represents youth and beauty and is the symbol of purity and innocence. The pearl is also said to have the highest personal vibration of any jewel; thus one must be a person of sensitivity and culture to love pearls truly, for when people of coarse and unrefined temperament possess a fine pearl for its monetary value only, trouble always follows. But for the fortunate, pearls bring better luck:

> Freedom from passion and from care
> If they the pearl will wear.

The gem as the symbol of health and long life is expressed in these couplets:

> Who comes with summer to this earth
> And owes to June her day of birth,
> With ring of pearl upon her hand
> Can health, long life, and wealth command.

As the June birthstone, this "aristocrat of gems" is considered one of the best possible gifts to a bride. It is also the most popular and occupies a very special place as one of the five precious jewels, bringing to its wearer both style and satisfaction. Its beauty is unique.

The pearl is the national gem of France, India, and the Philippines.

MOONSTONE

An opalescent, transparent gem, a variety of feldspar, the moonstone was so named because it contains bluish white spots which, when held to the light, present a silvery play of color not unlike that of the moon. It is generally cut in the form called cabochon, or round. One gemmologist has said: "It looks like a raindrop seen through a fine mist, at early dawn." The stone is colorless and translucent; light gleams from beneath its surface in a soft sheen that fades into pearl-like shadow. It possesses a "serene, mysterious beauty."

Not all moonstones, however, have this pearly cast. Some are tinted with green and blue, others with yellow, seemingly sprinkled all over with golden spots. The brilliant silvery rays and reflections seem to move around when the gem is turned back and forth, appearing like moonbeams playing over water. The moonstone is not at all expensive. It is a very feminine gem, looking equally well set in gold, silver, or platinum, but it is seldom used in ring settings because of its softness.

Moonstone has been found in the Alps, particularly in the Saint Gotthard district in south central Switzerland. The best stones of today are obtained in Ceylon from the gem gravels of streams. A yellow form is found in Malagasy. New deposits were uncovered in south India in the early 1950's; a supervisor discovered them in pebbles used in mixing concrete for construction work. These have proved to be superior stones, and diggings have been made to a depth of six to eight feet. Some show the quality called asterism, the optical illusion of a four-pointed star, caused by reflected light or transmitted light.

Synthetic moonstones often fail to reproduce the translucent quality of the genuine stones, though if set properly in jewelry this lack is not noticeable.

Quite naturally, this gem became associated with a great deal of superstition. The Romans believed that it enclosed the image of Diana, the moon goddess, who represented "the moonlight splendor of night," and it was supposed to have the power of bestowing victory, wealth, and wisdom on its wearer. Pliny maintained that the stone changed daily according to the waxing and waning of the moon, a belief held as late as the sixteenth century. Pope Leo X, one of the Medici family, was supposed to have owned a remarkable stone showing this change from brilliance to paleness. A story from the mid-sixteenth century tells of a stone about the size of a gold piece but thicker. A white point or marker grew larger or smaller as did the moon. The white mark first appeared at the top, and as it moved down to the center, like a small seed, it increased in size until, on reaching the middle, it was round like the full moon. The mark then gradually passed upward again as the moon waned. People of that day believed it acted as a love charm during the waxing of the moon; during the waning period, it would enable the wearer to foretell the future.

In India the stone is still considered sacred and brings good fortune. It is displayed for sale there only on a yellow cloth; yellow is a sacred color, the saffron orange-yellow color of Indian priests' robes. Indeed, it is supposed that a living spirit is inside the stone, a spirit leading to good luck.

As a gift for lovers, the moonstone is believed to arouse tenderness and to give the power to foretell good or ill fortune. To gain this knowledge, however, the stone must be placed in the mouth when the moon is full.

ALEXANDRITE

The unique feature of this transparent stone is that it possesses a dual color. In daylight it is a beautiful green, almost an emerald color, but in artificial light it becomes reddish-violet or violet. Lapidaries say that during the day it is an emerald and in the evening an amethyst. This chameleon among gemstones is therefore doubly enchanting.

The Alexandrite belongs to the mineral family of chrysoberyl. The word is often capitalized, for it was named in honor of Crown Prince Alexander of Russia—who became Czar Alexander II in 1855—when it was first discovered in the Ural Mountains in 1839 on the day when he became twenty-one. Since green and red were the Russian national colors, the stone attained an understandable popularity there.

It is quite uncommon and therefore very expensive, particularly those stones which possess a clear and easily noticed change of color. The green of the day, sometimes with a bluish cast, may be bold or possess a brownish tint. The purple has a reddish cast with a hint of orange, almost a raspberry or columbine red. If placed under a fluorescent lamp, it will immediately turn back to green.

The Alexandrite is rarely found in modern Russia, where the veins have been worked out, and the principal source has become Ceylon, where the stones are found in the pebbles of streams. Some have appeared, but only rarely, in both Brazil and Malagasy in localities where emeralds are mined. They are not generally as large as the Russian specimens, but their hardness makes it possible for them to be polished into great brilliance and to be cut to let the light play to the greatest possible extent.

Synthetic Alexandrites of good quality are now being produced, but they are based on the mineral composition of the sapphire. The change of light cannot be reproduced, however. These stones are of a reddish-purple, something like a reddish-hued amethyst with a tinge of green.

Quite naturally the most perfect specimens are in the Kremlin collection of the Russian crown jewels, for the czars succeeding Alexander exercised the royal prerogative of first choice of the stones from the mines in the Ural Mountains. Unfortunately, this collection has not been on view for over forty years, hence these prize examples cannot be seen. However, a sixty-six carat, record-size Alexandrite the colors of which range from green to red is on display in the Smithsonian Institution.

The day-and-night magic of this stone would probably have encouraged many of the kinds of superstitions surrounding other gems, except for the fact of comparatively recent discovery. In Russia it is believed to bring good luck.

CHAPTER 9

RUBY

JULY—CANCER (June 21–July 22)

Called the Lord of Gems, the ruby, still the rarest of
all stones, has always possesed an "other world" quality.
In the flowery language of ancient Eastern legends the
ruby was said to contain the original spark of life, described as "a deep drop of the heart's blood of Mother
Earth." Of both incomparable beauty and great rarity,
it is prized by many above the diamond. Author
John Ruskin called it "the loveliest stone of which I
have knowledge." The name is derived from the Latin
word *ruber*, "red." Since this was the name for all red
stones during the Middle Ages, the word ruby has been
much misused to label all red gems.

Ruby is a form of the mineral corundum, which is
normally drab and gray. Its color derives from chromium. It appears in six-sided crystals, and is the second
hardest of all gems, next to the diamond. This hardness
allows it to take and retain a high polish, and for this
reason the ruby is cut to bring out its brilliance of color
rather than shape. It is a heavy stone, and volume for
volume, is one-seventh heavier than the diamond.

Star rubies are those which contain a double refraction of light, brought out by cutting, which makes it
appear that a star of radiant white light is caught and

imbedded in the gem. This angle cut produces a single-rayed star due to the arrangement of crystals, and the impression is purely optical.

The finest and rarest rubies from Burma are called "pigeon's blood" and have a color which is intense rather than mixed or maroon. Others from Burma have a slight bluish tinge and are called the Burma rubies. Those from Thailand are dark red, sometimes brownish-red; the slightly paler rubies from Ceylon are like the pink sapphire.

The pigeon's blood rubies are found only in Mogok, Burma, either encased in limestone rock or in gem gravels. These mines have been in operation since the fifteenth century and are currently producing less and less. Those from Thailand are mined near Bangkok together with red spinel. Ceylonese rubies are becoming increasingly rare. To a lesser extent rubies are found in Queensland, Australia; and China, with a very limited production in the Ural Mountains of Russia. In the United States some have been found in North Carolina.

Since flawless rubies are increasingly rare, they are highly prized and expensive. The price may be from three to four thousand dollars a carat for the pigeon's blood type and from one hundred to one thousand dollars for less perfect stones of the other shades.

Fortunately, excellent synthetic stones are available at prices which are not prohibitive; otherwise the ordinary person would never see, much less own, a ruby. These artificial stones are almost perfect reproductions and can be identified only by specialists. The formula worked out by the French chemist Auguste Verneuil in the last decade of the nineteenth century produces perfect transparent crystals with the exact red shades, which when cut are indistinguishable from natural stones. Imitation glass rubies are less similar to the genuine stones.

Industrial rubies of nongem quality have been produced since the latter part of the eighteenth century and are used as movement bearings in fine watches. High quality phonograph needles—equal to industrial diamonds—are also made of rubies, and the synthetics are also used in parts of various scientific instruments. They form the heart of quantum generators in man-made satellites.

Because perfect rubies are so rare, the number of famous stones is smaller than one would expect. Ancient oriental writers tell of huge and dazzlingly beautiful stones, but these may for the most part refer to other less precious red gemstones and the stories may be considered legendary since few examples have survived. Certain it is that oriental rajahs and potentates possessed and enjoyed them. The first account of one actually being seen was made by Marco Polo who wrote that the finest ruby he saw on his travels was owned by the King of Ceylon: "It is a span [about nine inches] long, as thick as a man's arm, and without a flaw." The early-thirteenth-century Emperor of China, the Mongol Kublai Khan, offered "the value of a city" for it, said Polo, and the King answered that he would not part with it "if all the treasures of the world were laid at his feet." Since the Indian gem workers cut rubies to bring out their fire, this stone may possibly have come from there.

The thirteenth-century King of Siam owned a priceless ruby the size of a man's hand. Its owner believed that if held by him it had the power to prolong his youth. This may have been true, for every night and morning the King rubbed the stone over his face and neck as a regular ritual and when he died at the age of ninety he was said to have had the complexion of "a young man, unblemished and unwrinkled."

The Black Prince's Ruby, one of the British crown jewels, which was given to him by the King of Castile in 1367, bears that name incorrectly, for it has long been identified as a red spinel which is loosely called ruby.

Another misnamed spinel is the Timur, or Tribute of the World, Ruby, which was given to Queen Victoria in 1851; this is the largest ever known. It probably belonged to many rulers of India and Persia, for their names are carved in Arabic on the reverse side, the first being dated 1398. At one time it was owned by the Indian Shah Jaehan who built the Taj Mahal.

Genuine large rubies are less known. They undoubtedly still exist among the treasures of the rajahs of India but are held as heirlooms and are unpublicized.

The Edwardes Ruby in the British Museum was given by a Governor of India of that name in 1887 and weighs 167 carats, or about 1¼ ounces.

The best star ruby collection is in the American Museum of Natural History along with magnificent star sapphires. Said to be one of the largest of its kind is the Edith Haggin De Long Star, named in honor of the lady who presented it. From Burma, it weighs one hundred carats and is about one and one-half inches long and one inch wide. The stone is a milky crimson and its beautiful star is unusually well defined and brilliant.

The largest star ruby in the United States, weighing 138 carats, was presented to the Smithsonian Institution in 1965 by a New York advertising man, Rosser Reeves. It is insured for $150,000.

The rarity and incomparable beauty of the ruby has caused it to be connected with legends from the time of the ancient Orient to the present. Some of these first traditions were still current during the Middle Ages, and most of them refer to the pigeon's eye, which is synonymous with the oriental or true ruby.

In antiquity the stone was a token of friendship, the finest and most lavish gift which could be presented to another; this custom was followed in all ages and places. In India rubies were thought to possess caste: The deeper colors were of the highest caste; the paler the color, the lower in the caste structure. As in the human caste system the stones could lose both caste and the supernatural powers attached to them by coming in contact with pale stones of the lowest caste, the untouchables.

In the far-off past, the priest-kings of ancient dynasties considered the ruby to be the stone of devotion. Even in modern church rings the stone is used in uncut form to indicate glory.

The ancient Orientals dwelt at length on the fact that the ruby was self-luminous. For that reason it was called the "glowing stone" or "lamp stone," and an emperor of China "had in his chamber in one of the pillars of gold a ruby half a foot in length, that in the night seemeth so large and clear and shining that it is as light as day." Brahman traditions describe the home of the gods as lighted by enormous rubies and emeralds. A much later Greek legend tells of Heraclea and a lame female stork to which she had been very kind. To show her appreciation the stork brought in her beak and put in her mistress's lap a ruby of such surpassing brilliance that Heraclea used it to light up her room at night.

The Romans considered the ruby to be the stone of the war god Mars; as a strong color it was particularly appropriate to a man since it signified command, nobility, power, and vengeance.

As a stone of good luck the ruby gave courage and held a magic which always brought success. No matter how dangerous the task, the ruby was sure to give victory. At the time of the Crusades it was a favorite talisman and love token. Many a gallant knight rode to war against the infidels wearing his lady's heart in the shape of a ruby. King Henry V of England wore a magnificent ruby at the crucial Battle of Agincourt, and it proved to be a stone of success for him.

Perhaps the height of the ruby's powers was attained during the Middle Ages when superstitions were rife and gems were widely employed by soothsayers and makers of potions. One medieval belief concerned its

change of color. The ruby was thought to be able to pre-
dict misfortune, illness, or death to its possessor by becoming dark and losing its luster. Rubies turned dark
with the approach of ill fortune or danger and became
brilliant again when the future promised better things.
Another belief was that a ruby turned white when peril
threatened its wearer and regained its color when the
danger was passed. Like other red stones, the ruby was
used as a cure for bleeding.

Throughout its long history the ruby has always represented wealth and riches, even more so than the
other three precious stones. Without doubt this is due to
its continued rarity. The Bible is filled with references
to the ruby as the symbol of wealth. Job said, "The
price of wisdom is above rubies," and in Proverbs,
31:10, there appears: "Who can find a virtuous woman?
for her price is far above rubies."

Those born in July will enjoy the best, for their birthstone stands for love:

> The glowing ruby should adorn
> Those who in warm July are born,
> Then will they be exempt and free
> From love's doubt and anxiety.

The ruby is the national gem of Burma and Thailand.

CHAPTER 10

SARDONYX OR PERIDOT

AUGUST—LEO (July 23–August 22)

SARDONYX

Onyx is a banded form of agate, one of the varieties of quartz. Everyone is familiar with agate, particularly in the form of petrified wood; any boy who plays marbles considers his "aggies" as his prizes, even though most of them are made of glass. In sculpture, agate is called marble and its chief characteristic is that it takes a high polish which brings out the colors of the bands. Different names for agate are applied according to the color of the bands. The beauty of the stones depends upon the contrasting colors and transparency of these bands.

Sardonyx is found in parallel, alternate layers of reddish sand and onyx. Hence the name sardonyx. *Sard* is the Greek word meaning "reddish-brown," and *onyx* is a Latin word meaning "a veined gem." The brownish-red combined with white is best-known in the form of the cameo, with the figure cut in the white upper layer and the polished red-brown base forming the background. In some forms the onyx layer is a light pink. In the days when fob watches were in fashion, the stone at the end of the gold chain or ribbon was invariably sardonyx. Napoleon obtained a fine carved sardonyx in Egypt and wore it on his watch chain.

Like all varieties of agate, sardonyx is found as rounded boulders or pebbles or in broken fragments. It is relatively common and inexpensive. The best varieties are found in India. Some of the places where it is currently found are in the Idar-Oberstein section of Germany, in Czechoslovakia, Brazil, and Uruguay, as well as several parts of the United States, notably the Lake Superior region and Oregon.

Though glass imitations are available, sardonyx in cameos, rings, bookends, and the like is usually genuine because of the low price. It will probably be called onyx, the general term, but this variety is the only one which has the brown, or reddish brown, and white, or red and white.

The most famous sardonyx in history was set in a gold ring carved with a portrait of Queen Elizabeth I and given by her to her favorite, the Earl of Essex, as a token of their friendship. With it she assured him of her aid if ever he needed it. When the Earl was imprisoned for treason and condemned to be beheaded, he attempted to send the ring to the Queen but it fell into the hands of Lady Nottingham, whose husband was the sworn enemy of Essex, instead of his sister, who was to have delivered it to Elizabeth. Out of loyalty to her husband, Lady Nottingham did not give the ring to Elizabeth, and thinking Essex too proud to ask her mercy the Queen allowed him to be executed. When Lady Nottingham confessed her act on her deathbed, it broke the Queen's heart, and many believe that her remorse for the death of her former favorite caused Elizabeth's death a few weeks later. "The Queen brooded and pined for her lost lover, and the causes of her fading and giving up the will to live was well known among us though we could not speak of it." "She would fair swoon in her misery," wrote one of her ladies-in-waiting.

Josephine, Napoleon's Empress, possessed a superb necklace made of twelve antique sardonyxes engraved with classical subjects—gods, goddesses, and heroes—each surrounded with diamond brilliants and linked together by gold filigree encrusted with small pearls.

As one of the favorite ancient gems, sardonyx is included in all museum collections of Egyptian, Roman, and Greek stones. These stones are generally carved.

The reason for this stone's popularity among the ancients is readily understood when one realizes that many of the finest precious and semiprecious gems were in short supply and only available to royalty and the nobility. Sardonyx was available in quantity and with fine carving supplied attractive ornaments and seals. As long as four thousand years ago, the Egyptians cut them as sacred scarabs, or beetles, and since they present their best colors when flat, they were much in demand as talismans to be worn around the neck.

The early Hebrews wore sardonyx on their persons and used it in their temple decorations; it was the first stone in the breastplate of the Hebrew High Priest Aaron. The Greeks and Romans used the stone extensively as seals. Cameos first attained their popularity during these classical periods, and the exploits of the ancient gods and heroes as well as the rulers were carved on them. One of the most perfect of all cameos, nine inches long and eight inches wide, portrays the coronation of the Emperor Augustus; this is one of the largest ever to come to light.

The Romans believed strongly in talismans, objects bearing a sign or character engraved under astrological influence and thought to act as charms to avert evil and bring good fortune. Roman soldiers wore as talismans the sardonyx engraved with a figure of the hero Hercules or Mars, the god of war, hoping the stone would make its wearer as brave and daring as the carved figure.

In the Middle Ages the sardonyx was believed to possess healing powers. As one of the agate family, along with the opal, it was used as an eyestone to be applied directly on the lids. Its effectiveness may have been due to the fact that the agate is cold to the touch and may have furnished some relief. Another use was to protect the wearer from infections and poisons, including the bites of snakes and insects.

During the Renaissance other powers were attributed to the stone. It was supposed to confer the power of eloquence on the wearer and was therefore valuable to public speakers and orators. Bashful lovers might also be able to express the depth of their devotion when wearing it. A romantic lady was said to be able to capture the object of her admiration, for the stone was "of incalculable aid" in charming him. The stone also symbolized married happiness, and every wife, it was said, should follow this advice:

Wear a sardonyx or for thee
No conjugal felicity.
The August-born without this stone
'Tis said must live unloved and lone.

PERIDOT

The alternate August natal stone offers a contrast to the sardonyx in its brightness. It is of an unusual green, yellow-green, and olive-green color which is similar to the topaz. Though popular in ancient times, it is comparatively rare today because it is only found in quantity in one place, the island of Zeberged, also called St. John's Island, in the Red Sea, an Egyptian possession. Yet it is one of the most beautiful of all semiprecious stones. It is also one of the few gems that occur in nature in one color only. The peridot is the present national gem of Egypt.

A variety of the mineral olivine, it is often confused with the green garnet and other green stones. The particular shade of olive or bottle green is unique. A clear and transparent stone, it can be cut to bring out a brilliance equal to that of any other semiprecious stone. It is a magnesium-iron silicate, the magnesium accounting for the green color. It is not as expensive as might be thought.

In Burma, Ceylon, Australia, Norway, and Mexico, a less beautiful color has been found in yellow-green. Stones from the Red Sea island are becoming increasingly rare, because the French syndicate which owns the rights on this barren desert island takes a mining crew there only when the worldwide stock of the peridot is low. All supplies must be carried with them; even the drinking water has to be brought from the mainland of Egypt, fifty miles away. After a few months of operation the mines are again closed down until sales have reduced the stockpile. Peridots have also been found in meteorites.

The gemmologists Richard Pearl, Professor of Geology at the University of Colorado, and Frederick Pough, one of our country's best-known gem authorities, who was for many years in charge of the great Morgan Collection of gems at the American Museum of Natural History in New York, have called attention to the occurrence of peridot in volcanic rocks in Arizona and New Mexico. Ants are the miners of the insect world there. "The tiny peridot pebbles which withstand weathering better than the surrounding rock," says Dr. Pough, "are scattered throughout the area. As the ants tunnel through the area (in excavating their nests), the pebbles block their way. The ants push the pebbles out onto a waste pile, the anthill, where anyone can pick them up." These are not of course, the fine, large stones suitable for jewelry.

The finest stone has the quality possessed by Alexandrite: It shows to better advantage in artificial light. Such a specimen is known as the "evening emerald" because it then becomes a darker green. Because of its comparative softness it is unsuitable for use in rings. In a brooch or necklace or as earrings it excels because of its unusual magic color, and it was one of the favorite gems in Victorian England.

The peridot is one of the oldest known stones. The "topaz" in the breastplate of Aaron was probably this gem; Pliny, the first of the gemmologists, confused it with the green topaz. In Egypt, where they undoubtedly were obtained from the Red Sea mines worked by slaves about 1500 B.C., peridots were well known and prized for their unusual color.

The Crusaders, thinking they were emeralds, brought stones back to Europe and gave them to churches, where they were an essential feature of ornament during the Middle Ages.

The largest specimen in existence today, of 310 carats, is a part of the Smithsonian Institution collection. Another outstanding peridot, a crystal-clear stone of a fine olive-green color, weighing 192 carats, is in the Kremlin collection of the Russian crown jewels.

Perhaps because of its rarity, few superstitions are associated with the peridot. The Romans wore it to "repel terror, enchantment and melancholie." In the Middle Ages it was a charm against "the evil spirits of the night"—fear of the "evil eye" and a terror of darkness were common then. When pierced and strung on the hair of an animal or attached to the left arm it was thought to serve as a protection against the effects of evil spirits. King Edward VII of England chose it as his talisman.

> Though Leo's sign it is quite well
> To free yourself from evil spell,
> For in this gem surcease doth dwell.

CHAPTER 11

SAPPHIRE

SEPTEMBER—VIRGO (August 23–September 22)

Called by the Persians the Celestial Stone, the sapphire is popularly thought of as a stone of blue only. This is not true, but the term *blue* has come to be synonymous with sapphire, and the finest stones from Kashmir and Burma are of a color like the sky:

> The color of the air as seen on high
> When not a cloud obscures the sky.

The name in the Hebrew, Sanskrit, and Persian languages means "the stone of Saturn." Our word apparently has several sources: the Arabic *safir;* the Greek word *sappheiros,* which refers to the Sappherine Island in the Arabian Sea where it was found in ancient Grecian times; and the Latin word *sapphirus.* In ancient times the sapphire was called lapis lazuli, but the modern stone of that name, the alternate birthstone for September on the British list, is a different stone of a deep-blue color.

Sapphire is a mineral corundum, the red variety of which is ruby. It is aluminum, with the color added by iron and titanium. Of a six-sided crystal formation, it is similar to the ruby in being of a hardness second only to the diamond, and can be highly polished and cut to show a double brilliance.

Star sapphires, called asterias, are identical with star rubies except in color. They show the reflections of the long needles or tubes to form a six-pointed star. The best are deep blue with enough cloudiness to make the rays stand out.

In addition to the traditional blue shade which varies from clear to pale, natural sapphires occur in many colors and tints, including yellow, pink, violet, orange, and blue-green. Excellent synthetic stones are produced which are difficult to distinguish from the genuine, but the synthetic stars are rare, being tinted quartz. Sapphires are used industrially in the movements of fine watches, scientific apparatus, and phonograph needles.

Sapphires are mined in shallow hand-dug pits, for they occur near the surface. Kashmir was long the source of the finest cornflower blue stones, but the recent output is of inferior quality. Ceylon, Burma, and Australia produce blues—Ceylon, royal and pale; Burma, deep blue; and Australia, an inky deep blue— as well as stones of various other colors. In the United States the Yogo Gulch Mine in Montana, the largest gem mine in the country, produces both blue and other colors, but the stones are small and used largely for industrial purposes. The best star sapphires are from Ceylon.

Sapphires vary greatly in price. They are not as expensive as their sister rubies, except for the cornflower blues from Kashmir and Burma, and the excellent synthetics are quite inexpensive. Women prefer them in rings or set in platinum with diamonds. Sapphires are particularly suitable for men when set in platinum and worn on the little finger of the left hand; they are used also in cuff links and shirt studs in formal wear.

Sapphires are a regular part of museum collections, but only a few of the flawless cornflower blues are on display since those available are quickly sold.

Two sapphires of historical importance are among the British crown jewels in the Tower of London. St. Edward's Sapphire, so-called because it was originally mounted in a ring worn by Edward the Confessor at his coronation in 1042, appears in the cross of the Imperial State Crown made for Queen Victoria in 1838 and is the oldest gem in it. This is not the crown presently worn. The Stuart or Charles II's Sapphire is at the back of the present state crown. It measures one and one-half inches in length and one inch in breadth and has been moved several times to be replaced by some of the priceless South African diamonds and other precious stones received from the colonies in the later years of the nineteenth century.

The British Museum possesses several excellent sapphires. The Russian crown jewels in the Kremlin include some fine blue sapphires, one an oval-shaped stone of 260 carats. The last Czarina of Russia, Empress Alexandra, possessed a collection of her favorite cornflower blues from Ceylon. One of her diadems contained several large pear-shaped and oval sapphires. One of her jeweled aigrettes, shaped like a feather, had five large and seventy-five small sapphires mixed with diamonds; this was mounted on fine wires so that with the slightest movement they quivered and shone with hypnotic effect. All these sapphires disappeared during the Russian Revolution.

The late Queen Mary, the wife of King George V and grandmother of the present Queen Elizabeth II, was a collector of sapphires. One of her favorite pieces of jewelry was a necklace of thirty-four perfectly matched blues from Ceylon.

The largest blue sapphire, called the Gem of the Jungle, was found in Burma in 1929; weighing 958 carats, it was cut into nine large stones which were sold to millionaires.

The Morgan Collection of the American Museum of Natural History is considered the world's finest collection of sapphires and rubies. Its notable sapphires are a blue of 163 carats and a yellow of 100 carats, a 34-carat violet from Burma, and a golden yellow of 75 carats. Included in this museum's collection is the Star of India, from Ceylon, which weighs 565 carats, or almost four ounces, and is the largest and most perfect. This stone was stolen with eight other sapphires in a daring robbery in October, 1964, and recovered in Miami in 1965. The other prize Ceylonese star sapphire, the Midnight Star, is a deep purple and weighs 116 carats. These were all the gifts of the financier J. P. Morgan. The second largest star sapphire in the United States is the 330-carat Star of Asia in the Smithsonian Institution.

Four of the most remarkable of all sapphires, one black and three blue-black, are on display in the Smithsonian Institution in Washington, D.C., to which they were recently donated by two brothers, Harry and James Kazanjian, Los Angeles gem dealers, in tribute to the opportunities America had offered to them. The stones have been carved with the heads of four presidents—Washington, Jefferson, Lincoln, and Eisenhower. The Lincoln dark-blue sapphire is the largest known in the world, weighing 1,318 carats—over nine ounces. It was from an Australian mine. The head is two and three-fifths inches high, one and three-fourths inches wide and two inches deep. The other stones are somewhat smaller.

The traditions surrounding the sapphire refer to its color. It was and is considered the most spiritual of all gems, representing the purity of the soul. This belief recurs in all periods and involves particularly chastity and the factors in a good and pure life. Since it mirrors the blue of the heavens, this symbolism is easily understood.

The sapphire of the ancients was called lapis lazuli until the Greeks gave it the name it now bears. In the Hebrew High Priest's breastplate it was the fifth stone, in the center of the second row, and it was the second stone in the foundations of the New Jerusalem. A writer in the Pentateuch called it "the body of heaven in its clearness."

The sapphire was the gem of Apollo, the Greek god of prophecy, and was to be worn by those who visited his shrine at Delphi to seek his aid. Several Roman gods and goddesses—Jupiter, Saturn, and Venus—were associated in one way or another with this stone.

Before and during the Middle Ages, the sapphire was a priestly gem. Since it was the symbol of purity, it would prevent "impure thoughts" and evil in priests and protect them from the temptations of the flesh; it would "quell the animal senses." During the thirteenth and fourteenth centuries, popes, cardinals, and bishops wore rings set with sapphires because the pure-blue color was symbolic of the heavens.

The common man shared in its good moral effect; it was said to be "a great help in leading a good life." When warriors had to leave their young wives, they would give them necklaces of genuine sapphires so that they would remain true. The color would darken if worn by an adulterer or adulteress, even as it would change color if worn by an "unworthy" person.

An additional quality was protection against snakes. The sapphire's power was thought to be so great that if a poisonous reptile or spider were placed in a jar with the stone it would immediately die. A monk writing in Latin in 1260 gave this hint for snake fighters: "Its virtue is contrary to venom and quencheth it. If thou put an adder in a box and hold a sapphire at the mouth, by virtue thereof the adder is overcome and dieth, as it were suddenly. And this same I have seen proved in many and divers places."

The eyes also would receive great help from sapphires. Diseases would be immediately cured. Used as an eyewash to remove foreign bodies, a sapphire should be dipped in cold water both before and after the operation.

Its medieval healing properties extended far beyond the eyes. Powdered and taken internally with milk, it was considered an excellent remedy for "pestilence, poison, fever and hysteria." It could expel "hot humours of the body." If placed over the heart, it would "bestow strength and energy." And boils from the plague could be made to disappear. The procedure for this was that a gem of fine, deep color should be selected and rubbed gently and slowly around the tumor. After the stone was removed recovery would follow because the sapphire would "continue to extract the pestilential virulency and contagious poison from the infected part."

Mental difficulties could also be healed:

> A maiden born when autumn leaves
> Are rustling in September's breeze
> A sapphire on her brow should bind,
> 'Twill cure diseases of the mind.

The remarkable coldness to the touch also gave rise to the idea that a sapphire could quench fires.

The sapphire has always been the symbol of truth and sincerity. The three cross rays of the star sapphire represented faith, hope, and love.

Fortunate, therefore, are those born in September with the generous powers of their natal stone.

The sapphire is the national gem of Greece.

CHAPTER 12

OPAL OR TOURMALINE
OCTOBER—LIBRA (September 23–October 22)

OPAL

This semiprecious stone is an October birthstone on both the American and British lists. Of all birthstones, the opal has been the subject of the most controversy. Gemmologists, collectors, and lovers of beauty agree on its almost unearthly loveliness. Yet no stone has varied more in popularity and acceptance; its reputation for bad luck has at times caused it to be shunned by believers in the influence of gems, and this tradition, at its height at the beginning of this century, has persisted for many years.

The name opal is of Sanskrit origin and means "stone" or "jewel." One of the mineral gems—silica, with a small part of water—opal is a soft stone, and both heat and pressure will cause variations in its colors.

In addition to the milk-white type with the unique opaqueness, which is characteristic of all varieties, those of color are called "fire" opals, meaning that the various cracks in the gemstone reflect a play of iridescent colors. Scientists have not yet agreed on the exact cause of this phenomenon, which produces an almost unparalled beauty. The "flash-fire" type has a large pattern which shows a single pattern when moved. The rarest and most beautiful type is called harlequin because the colors—red, yellow, blue, and green—occur in checks or squares like the clown's costume. "Black" opals, found in iron deposits, flash green, red, and blue.

In Roman times the stone was much prized, and Pliny, wrote this poetic description of the fire opal: "It is made up of the glories of the most precious stones. To describe it is a matter of inexpressible difficulty: There is in it the gentler fire of the ruby, the brilliant purple of the amethyst, the sea-green of the emerald, all shining together in an incredible union." In the Victorian period, the author John Ruskin said, "The opal, when pure, presents the most lovely colors that can be seen in the world, except those of clouds." So unmatchable is the beauty of this stone that no synthetic opals have been made.

Four major modern sources exist. The oldest is Hungary, where "wood" opals—trees changed to silica combined with water—were first found. The fire opal was first mined in Mexico; this reddish-yellow variety is unique in that the colors fade if the gem becomes moist. In our country, Nevada has produced fire opals considered second to none in brilliancy, showing deep flashes of reds, greens, and purples; these are wood opals formed from imbedded twigs and branches. The principal source, however, has been Australia, where, since they were first discovered in 1905, the best specimens have been mined. They occur in all mineral forms in the deserts of New South Wales, Queensland, and South Australia. From sunken shafts, the miners seek the rock cavities containing fiery specks.

Until the growth of the superstition of bad luck, opals were much prized by their owners. The Roman Senator Nonius owned a particularly gorgeous specimen about as large as a filbert nut, the modern value of which is estimated to be a million dollars. At that time Mark Antony was infatuated with Cleopatra, and he was determined to obtain the stone for a gift to her. When Nonius refused to part with it, he was exiled from Rome, with the loss of his property. But he took his prize with him. The finest opal in more modern times was owned by Josephine, Napoleon's empress. So flashing and vivid were the red lights in the gem that it was called "The Burning of Troy." This opal disappeared without a trace after Napoleon's downfall.

Some of the best opals in American museums are those from Nevada, included in the Morgan Collection of the American Museum of Natural History. One of these, of the wood type, is a polished slab 4 by 2½ by ¾ inches, with outstanding streaks of fire; it has an unusual history. In the early part of this century this fire opal was left with the proprietor of the general store in a Nevada mining encampment by an old prospector in return for a "grubstake"—supplies and money furnished on promise of a share in his discoveries. The prospector took his supplies and followed the "rainbow lure of the opal." He never returned— in fact, he was never again heard from—and his pledge, purchased by the financier and collector John P. Morgan, is now called "the Grubstake Opal."

Opals have been viewed with reverence from ancient times. The unique color radiations have served to surround them with an air of mystery. An Indian legend tells how the gods Brahma, Vishnu, and Shiva once vied in jealous love for a beautiful woman. This angered the Eternal, who changed the fair mortal into a creature made of mist. Thereupon each of the three gods endowed her with his own color so as to be able to recognize her. Brahma gave her the glorious blue of the heavens, Vishnu enriched her with the splendor of gold, and Shiva lent her his flaming red. But all this was in vain, since the lovely phantom was whisked away by the winds. Finally, the Eternal took pity on her and transformed her into a stone, the opal, that sparkles in all the colors of the rainbow.

The Orientals considered opals to be "the anchor of hope." The Arabians believed that they fell from the sky. In Roman days, the opal was called the "Cupid stone" because its tint suggested the clear complexion of the God of Love.

A high point in acceptance was reached during the Middle Ages, when opals began to be found in abundance in Hungary. The name became *ophthalmioe,* or eye stone, because when wrapped in a bay leaf it was supposed to sharpen the eyesight. It was believed by Poles to make an individual invisible; by wearing it thieves could carry away plunder in broad daylight —hence the name "the thief stone." This belief persisted even into the Elizabethan period in England.

The medieval period was one in which superstition flourished and astrology and sorcery was practiced. Because of the luminous appearance of the white opal and the color changes of the fire varieties, all sorts of influences were attributed to the opal in both health and human characteristics. The changes in the intensity of its colors were said to be due to whether the wearer enjoyed perfect health or was ill. The catalog of its effects included the strengthening of the heart, prevention of fainting, protection against infection, and the cleansing and sweetening of foul air. A blond woman, it was said, should wear an opal to preserve her hair color. A wearer would be relieved from dejection and always enjoy hope; in fact, the stone was the symbol of hope.

The belief regarding the opal as the bearer of bad luck first began in Europe during the plague called the Black Death in the mid-fourteenth century, in which a fourth of the population died. The gem was considered fatal to its wearer since, when worn by a patient, it was brilliant up to the point of death, and lost its luster thereafter. The stone was therefore assumed to be the cause of death; the truth, however, was that the death of the wearer caused the alteration because the change of temperature from fever heat to the chill of death affected the sensitive stone. Nevertheless, the opal's popularity suffered and it became a gem of dread.

Opals were treasured in Elizabethan England both for their power over the eye and their beauty. Shakespeare considered the gem the symbol of inconstancy because of its changing colors and included such references in several of his plays, including *Twelfth Night*.

As has been described, the superstition that the opal

is a gem bringing bad luck to the owner and wearer developed from the changes which take place in some varieties of this soft stone because of its structure. The cracks which give the gem its peculiar glow make it liable to damage, for it will often shatter along these lines. Heat from even a small amount of friction will cause it to split. Too much heat may make it shrink and consequently fall from its setting. Yet, although even constant body heat may shrink it, it must be worn frequently to retain its luster, for when it becomes cold it is dull and lifeless. As one of the softest of the semiprecious gems, with a hardness of 6½, it can be damaged beyond repair by scratches. Therefore an owner might quite naturally consider himself unlucky at times. In addition, unscrupulous jewelers often moisten poor quality opals with oil to bring out beautiful colors which disappear when the stone dries, after it has been purchased. Also, in displaying an opal, a jeweler often holds the opal in his palm because body heat enhances its color.

Most authorities agree that part of the opal's unpopularity grew from an 1829 novel by Sir Walter Scott, *Anne of Geierstein,* in which the Lady Hermione was never seen in public without an opal in her hair. Only when her servants dressed her hair was it laid aside, at which time she immediately lost her usual liveliness and spirit. When it was returned to its place, she was once again both gracious and filled with vitality. The gem seemed to give off its colors according to Hermione's moods. It sparkled when its owner was in a happy mood; it flamed red or green with her anger or jealousy. Her fear that it might be ruined if liquid touched it caused a wicked rival to accuse her publicly of witchcraft. Although Hermione's husband scoffed at the idea, he finally decided to sprinkle a little "holy water" on her forehead as a precaution. A drop fell on the opal. It shot one brilliant flash "like a falling star" and in an instant was as dull as a common pebble. Hermione fell lifeless on the chapel floor, and both she and the stone became a small heap of ashes.

Although Scott did not name the stone, the mention of its wonderful play of color and sensitivity to heat and moisture seemed to identify it to readers as the opal. British jewelers found immediately after the publication of *Anne of Geierstein* that opals were unsalable. And the superstition persisted until the discoveries of the opal deposits in Australia. The opal was a favorite stone of Queen Victoria. She brought it back to popularity by giving opals to each of her daughters when they were married, as well as to many of her friends, her object being, no doubt, to benefit her Australian subjects. Because fashion followed royalty, opals regained their former popularity.

Another story, true rather than fictional, was the much publicized experience of King Alfonso XII of Spain, whose rule, from 1874 to 1885, was comparatively short. The opal he possessed certainly brought more than his share of bad luck and sorrow.

As a young prince in exile, Alfonso fell in love with the beautiful Countess de Castiglione, whom he assured would become his queen when he became of age and ascended to the throne. But when he was crowned king in 1874, at seventeen, he jilted her to marry a princess of royal blood. Resolving on revenge, the Countess sent Alfonso "in memory of the old friendship" a wedding present of a superb opal set in a filigree ring of gold. This he gave to his wife, and her death from a mysterious illness occurred a few months afterward. The King then gave the ring to his grandmother, the Dowager Queen Christina, who died within a few years. Alfonso next presented the opal to his sister, the Infanta, who died within a year. The next recipient, his sister-in-law, wore the ring for several years before her death. Determined to break the evil spell, Alfonso began to wear the ring himself, but was soon struck down by a mysterious ailment, which caused his death when he was only twenty-seven. After these calamities, his successor, the Queen Regent, attached the ring to a chain of gold and hung it around the neck of a statue one of the patron saints of Madrid, the Virgin of Alumdena, where it may still be seen in the Catredal de Nuestra Señora de la Alumdena.

The explanation for this succession of royal deaths, however, lies not in the opal but in the fact that a plague of cholera was raging in Spain during Alfonso's reign. Over 100,000 died in one year, and the disease attacked all classes from peasant to royalty. The opal was still blamed, however, and its reputation and popularity continued to suffer.

For some inexplicable reason, the ill repute of the opal persists. The finest types, like the black, are expensive, and a woman deciding whether to buy a stone recalls its reputation, however unfounded, and cannot fail to wonder whether the stone will lose its luster or shrink in time. The risk involved is therefore considerable. Prices vary with types and cuts, from as little as ten dollars for small stones, to a thousand dollars or more for exceptionally beautiful specimens. As supplies decline, the prices are increasing. The beauty of the opal, however, is still a joy to the owner and wearer.

And, of course, there is always the hope and consolation expressed in these couplets:

> October's child is born for woe,
> And life's vicissitudes must know;
> But lay an opal on her breast,
> And hope will lull those woes to rest.

TOURMALINE

This alternate October birthstone is generally little known. Yet two of its characteristics—the variety of colors and its magnetic properties—make it unusual among semiprecious stones. However, because of its similarity to other gems and because it was not discovered until the eighteenth century and is therefore new in comparison with other stones, the tourmaline has no ancient folklore like the other birthstones. Many gemmologists believe that the tourmaline should not have a place on birthstone lists because it is so comparatively new, but those who prefer a bright gem without the associations related to the opal will be glad to examine the gem called the rainbow stone, and to wear it.

The origin of the name is Singhalese. The first known tourmalines were sent to Holland from Ceylon, where it was called *toramalli* which means "carnelian," a variety of chalcedony, which they thought it was. It is a complex silicate combined with various metals, each of which contributes to a different color and often leads to its being incorrectly recognized as another gem, such as ruby, emerald, or sapphire. However, tourmaline lacks the sharp brightness of these stones.

The particular quality—and its principal appeal to the buyer—is the wide variety of colors: yellow, green, red, blue, pink, brown, and black. These are due to the particular minerals in which tourmalines are found. The diversity is truly astounding, and some stones are bicolored; those of pink and green are particularly attractive. The combinations occur in mineral belts. The red stone resembling the ruby is called rubellite; the green, resembling the emerald is called the Brazilian Emerald and is the national gem of Brazil. The red from Siberia is called the Siberian Ruby. The crystals are usually found in granite, gneiss, or limestone, and are difficult to mine. For this reason large stones are extremely valuable.

One of the dazzling of all gems is the unique tourmaline known as "watermelon." The outer edge is green, with a transparent white zone surrounding the interior pink or light-red zone; the whole looks like a piece of watermelon. This type comes from Brazil.

The main sources at present are Brazil, for green and

blue; Ceylon; Malagasy; South Africa, for dark blue; and the states of Maine and California.

The principal discovery of the tourmaline was in 1820, in Maine, where two amateur boy-geologists returning from a collecting trip found a glittering crystal at the base of a tree. Later they found many more, and eventually more than $50,000 worth of gems was taken from this rock. Still later, tourmaline was found in California.

The gem's unusual electric properties and magnetic powers were first discovered by Dutch children in 1703. Playing with some crystals, they discovered that small bits of paper, lint, and ash were attracted to them. The cause was that when tourmaline is warmed or rubbed, it becomes charged with electricity. In his early study of electricity, Benjamin Franklin used tourmaline stones. At one time they were popular with amateur parlor magicians. The electric property makes them valuable for use in pressure gauges.

The major famous tourmaline was the pink-red stone presented to Russian Empress Catherine the Great by King Gustavus III of Sweden in 1777. Long thought to be a ruby, it was the size of a pigeon's egg, and is now in the Kremlin collection. The champagne 173-carat stone in the Smithsonian Institution is considered the most perfect tourmaline in the United States.

References to the tourmaline are comparatively rare. However, Helen Hunt Jackson, the author of *Ramona,* wrote a short story titled "My Tourmaline," set in Maine. A little girl finds a crystal lodged in the roots of a tree—like the original discoverers—and sprains her leg while removing it. During a subsequent six-week period in bed, she places the stone against her cheek in a silk bag, and can feel its prickling, tickling sensation which brings on sleep.

Miss Jackson's little girl in the story was unconsciously using a supposed medical power of the stone first discovered by a Dutch scientist in the eighteenth century, when the gem's electric properties were being investigated. Describing its effect on a child, he wrote, "when it [a tourmaline] is placed in the little silken bag that has been made to hold it, and is laid against her cheek, her feverish restlessness gradually disappears and gives place to tranquil sleep . . . . More than that she was aware of a species of subconscious sympathy with the stone."

One student has termed the gem the "peace stone," since it supposedly dispels fears and makes its wearer calm. Another maintains that a dream of tourmaline foretells an accident. Still another recommends the green variety as particularly good for people engaged in business, since it is supposed to attract success. According to one writer, the pink brings love and liking from those around the wearer, and this writer adds, "If you ever find yourself in a place where you are unpopular, acquire a pink tourmaline."

Tourmalines, with their bright colors, provide attractive contrasting color to a dress.

A purchaser should know that what a jeweler calls by other names—the Brazilian emerald, the Brazilian peridot, the Brazilian sapphire, and the peridot of Ceylon—are tourmalines. For those born in October, these stones may be preferable to the opal both in price and color.

CHAPTER 13

TOPAZ

NOVEMBER—SCORPIO (October 23–November 21)

The general impression of the topaz is that it is a yellow or golden-hued gemstone. Though this type is called by jewelers "the precious topaz," the truth is that the gem appears in many colors. Few stones have been the subject of more confusion because less-expensive semiprecious stones can easily be passed off as topazes.

Confusion also exists about the origin of the gem's name. The word is of Eastern derivation, the Sanskrit *topaz* meaning "fire"; *top* denoting "to shine." We get the English word from the Greek *topazos,* "to seek and find," but minerologists consider this name source to be questionable. However, Pliny used it in describing an island in the Red Sea called Topazos that was almost always surrounded by fog and was therefore difficult for sailors to find; he also confuses topaz with chrysolite, which is often incorrectly identified as topaz. The foggy island, now called Zeberged or St. John's Island, is the major source of August's alternate birthstone, peridot, with which it is also often incorrectly identified, and was supposedly guarded by a chosen few whose duty was to keep people from landing. Even those who were given permission to go ashore were not allowed to see the gems in daylight, for it was only after nightfall that they were said to show their great radiance. When the Greek seamen saw their first specimens there after penetrating the fog, they christened the land Topazos and the gem *topazos*, "sought and found."

The name topaz is unfortunately currently misused to identify many stones, and the semiprecious stone citrine which is inexpensive and very popular is passed off as topaz. The genuine or "precious" topaz is neither common nor widely used in modern jewelry because of its rarity and cost.

The real, transparent topaz is a silicate composed of quartz crystals in aluminum. The vapors of fluorine gas which have passed through the rocks have changed the mineral into topaz.

The colors are of an endless variety extending from clear white through the entire color spectrum to black. These include red, blue, green, and yellows and browns. Oscar Wilde described those in his collection in these words: "I have topazes as yellow as the eyes of tigers, topazes as pink as the eyes of wood pigeons and green topazes that are as the eyes of cats."

The extremely rare brown stones, ranging from a rich pink-brown to red-brown but principally showing a clear golden color, are found only in southern Brazil and in several localities in Russia. The popular blue stones, resembling the aquamarine, come principally from Ceylon and Japan. They are a light watery blue which fades in daylight, and the excellent collection in the British Museum is therefore always kept in darkness. The colorless variety is often confused with the diamond and sold as "white sapphire." It is obtained mainly from gravel beds in Brazil, where it is called in Portuguese *pingos de água*, "drops of water."

A synthetic variety from Brazil is pink in color; the deep-yellow stones are slowly and carefully heated until they attain the perfect desired color, and are sold as "pinked" stones. Those from Spain, called Spanish topaz, are amethysts which are heated to a yellow color approaching that of the precious topaz.

In addition to the countries mentioned above, topazes are also mined in India and Ceylon, Germany, Scotland, Mexico, parts of Africa, and many areas in the United States, particularly Colorado, Maine, New Hampshire, and Utah.

Topaz occurs in a wide variety of sizes, but the biggest accumulations—up to thirty pounds—are generally of poor quality. The largest uncut stone ever found is now in the gem collection of the American Museum of Natural History in New York City. It is from Brazil and weighs nearly six hundred pounds.

The finest topazes possess a lively fire. Because of their hardness they can be polished to superb brilliancy. However, flawless genuine stones of good color are scarce. The gem is used in rings, clips, necklaces, brooches, and bracelets.

The most famous topaz, incorrectly called the Braganza diamond, was one of the crown jewels of Portugal. This yellow stone was found there in 1740 and weighed 1,680 carats, or twelve ounces. A blue stone from Japan, the Morgenthau topaz in the American

Museum of Natural History, is considered to be one of the finest examples of gem cutting ever performed. In 1915 an expert worked a hundred hours to produce its 444 facets. The colorless topaz called the Maxwell Stuart was from Ceylon and when cut in 1897 weighed 270 carats, or nearly three ounces. The Smithsonian Institution possesses a 235 carat stone from Colorado. The largest topazes in its collection are a mammoth 7,725 carat yellow and a 3,273 carat blue, both from Brazil.

Throughout the ages the topaz has accumulated a lore equaling that of the most-valued gems. Indeed, November's child may quite properly become confused with the many attributes the stone has been said to possess.

In addition to being the tenth stone in the fourth row in Aaron's breastplate, topaz was the material of one of the gates of the New Jerusalem. Ancients considered it to be the stone of strength, deriving its powers from the sun. Thus is brought both wealth and power to the monarchs and princes who wore it.

The power attributed to the topaz during the Middle Ages was considerable. It would chill boiling water when put into it—the ruby's power in reverse. The medical uses were many. It could cure fevers and when powdered and added to wine would prevent asthma and insomnia. Diseases of the eye were guaranteed to disappear if powdered topaz was placed in wine for three days and nights and the resulting liquid rubbed on the eyes just before going to sleep. It could also stimulate the appetite, though the method by which this was achieved is not recorded. Held in the hand of a woman in childbirth, it was believed to lessen her suffering. A nonmedical medieval belief was that when worn set in gold in a necklace or on the left arm, "spells and enchantments" could be warded off.

Its most unusual power, mentioned during the Renaissance, was that of giving off light in the dark. A stone owned by a Dutch count was "known to give such a brilliant light throughout the chapel where it was kept that prayers could be read without the help of a lamp"!

The virtues of the topaz were many. It brought cheerfulness and pleasant dreams to the wearer, who would enjoy long life, beauty, and intelligence. It has always been the symbol of friendship.

> Who first comes to this world below
> With drear November's fog and snow
> Should prize the topaz's amber hue
> Emblem of friends and lovers true.

CHAPTER 14

TURQUOISE OR ZIRCON
DECEMBER—SAGITTARIUS
(November 22–December 21)

TURQUOISE

Perhaps the earliest known and used gemstone, the turquoise is not only one of the oldest gems found set in jewelry, but is undoubtedly among the best-known and most-worn in our country. Admirers of the crafts of the American Indian and travelers in Arizona, New Mexico, Nevada, Colorado, and California are very likely to buy jewelry set with turquoise.

The name of the stone in Iran, source of the finest stones—is *piruzeh*. But turquoises were first introduced into Europe by Turkish merchants, hence the name became *turchesa*, "The Turkish stone," from the term for the Turks, *Turkis*. The name used today is the French version of this—*pierre turquoise*, "stone of Turkey."

Turquoise is a soft, porous, opaque stone which is a combination of copper and aluminum when blue, and copper and iron when green. It is always imbedded in the veins of rocks, and is found near the surface.

The principal contemporary sources are in the desert lands of Iran and the American Southwest, though they have been found at various times in Egypt, Tibet, and Australia. In ancient times the Sinai mines of

Egypt, the oldest in the world, which have not been operating for the last three thousand years, were a major source. The early Egyptians thought highly of this gem, preferring it to all others, and the pharaohs used it extensively. The oldest pieces of jewelry in the world are four magnificent turquoise bracelets found in 1900 in the tomb of Queen Zer, who ruled about 5500 B.C. They were on her mummified arm wrapped in brown bandages.

Persia was the other ancient source, and the mines in the Iranian province of Khurasan still produce the most perfect turquoises available today. For ten centuries the deposits there have yielded the world's finest specimens, characterized by their pure-blue color and absence of porosity. With picks and crowbars, pieces of limestone and sandstone are chopped off and brought to the surface in buckets. There the fragments are broken by hammers, and the largest pieces of turquoise picked out. These Iranian stones are the most highly prized because they possess the rare and desirable sky-blue color.

The deposits in the American West and Southwest, mined by the American Indians before Columbus discovered America, were later operated by the Spanish conquerors. The turquoise has long been the favorite stone of Indian tribes. The Navajos are particularly skillful silversmiths, beating the silver to be used as mountings for turquoise buttons, beads, belt buckles, bracelets, rings, and necklaces, with designs of great beauty. The turquoise stones, both blue-green and green, are generally added by the Pueblo Indians of both Arizona and New Mexico.

Though the clear stones are considered the best, attractive low cost gems are veined with small strips of brown and black rock; these are sometimes speckled. Turquoise is soft and porous and tends to fade in color when the moisture within dries out. For that reason and because they have no natural luster, they are generally treated with wax to give them a sheen. Even the perspiration of a wearer, when absorbed by the stone, changes its color. The turquoise can sometimes be brightened by washing in ammonia.

The finest turquoise collection is in Iran, where it is the national gem. What is considered to be the best specimen in the world, without flaw, is about 3½ inches long, and is owned by the Shah. Still in the palace is a throne given to Shah Affas by the Russian Czar Boris Godunov in 1604. It is covered with 825 good-sized turquoises, 552 rubies, and 187 whole pearls—and was used at the coronation of Queen Farah in 1967. The Russian crown jewels included a diadem of lovely sky-blue turquoises and diamonds. The Morgan collection of the American Museum of Natural History displays a superb stone from Tibet carved with the Chinese Goddess of Mercy. The reason for the comparative lack of historical stones is that the color of the stone changes with age; only those mined in Iran retain the ideal clear blue.

Many of the superstitions surrounding the turquoise grew out of its tendency to fade or change color. An Arabian writing in the twelfth century explained this by saying, "The turquoise shines when the air is pure and becomes pale when it is dim." Another Arabian, a minerologist, claimed that the color changed according to the weather. But most of the beliefs were associated with illness. A treatise by a fifteenth-century philosopher stated that the change was due to the stone's ability to attract poisons: "The turquoise quickly destroys every poison, whether vegetable or arising within a living body." It could indicate the state of the wearer's health, turning pale when he became sick, losing its color when he died, and regaining its former beauty in the hands of a new and healthy owner. Hence the saying:

> The sympathizing turquoise true doth tell,
> By looking pale, the wearer is not well.

"Because of the fact that the turquoise changes color on the illness of the wearer and upon his death flies completely to pieces," a sixteenth-century physician wrote, "one concludes that the stone so sympathizes with the wearer that it suffers with him." Czar Ivan the Terrible of Russia was said to believe this.

The permanence of the blue color constituted a prediction of the weather. The Persians believed that when a turquoise was seen clearly in the morning, a happy and clear day would come to pass.

The stone changed, according to an eighteenth-century writer, "when there is any peril prepared for him that weareth it."

Its antipoison attribute applied particularly to the stings of scorpions "when administered as a potion." Furthermore, according to a fifteenth-century writer, "it quickly destroys every poison, whether vegetable or arising within a living body, or a mixture of both." It was also effective, we are told, in driving away those pains which result through "demoniacal or other evil influences." The Persians believed that the blue of the turquoise would overcome the effects of the "evil eye"; even today camels, horses, and mules in Iran often have blue beads attached to their tails; highly valued animals may wear necklaces. Human beings wearing the stone in any form are supposedly assured of this protection.

Another medical property was its effect on the eye, which was strengthened by merely looking at a turquoise. When an eye was inflamed, placing a stone against it would cure the difficulty. "By its application the eye increases its luster, prevents the fall of fluid therefrom, brings back the color of the pupil if it becomes white and even restores natural vision to those who are almost blind."

Another of its protective qualities, according to Persian writers, was to protect the wearer from injury by falling, especially from horseback; later this was extended to cover falls from a building or over a precipice. This was particularly valuable when riding on horseback, for the horse became more surefooted. Furthermore, a horse wearing a turquoise amulet would be protected from the ill effects resulting from drinking cold water when overheated by exertion.

The preference of the Indians of the Southwest for turquoise is explained by its availability, but may also be due to the fact that blue is their symbol for Heaven and green for Earth. So highly regarded is the stone that since the time of their ancestors of several thousand years ago it has been called by the name "Chalcui-hui-tal," which means "the highest and most valued thing in the world"; though other precious stones like opals, garnets, and rubies may be found in the region, the Indians have never used them and would not touch them, and no stone other than the turquoise is ever found in their homes or graves. The stone is considered to be a guardian of tombs. Indian medicine men worked their charms with turquoises, and warriors or hunters attached a stone to their bows to assure perfect aim.

In more modern times the turquoise was a love charm and considered a pledge of affection when received as a gift. If the loved one was unfaithful, it was believed the suitor would know because of the change in the stone's color. Lovers could be reconciled by wearing the stones. Leah, in Shakespeare's *Merchant of Venice*, gave a turquoise ring to Shylock "when he was a bachelor" in order to win his love and get him to propose to her. In Russia the stone is common in wedding rings. Faithfulness in love is assured for the turquoise wearer:

> The heav'n-blue turquoise should adorn
> Those who are in December born;
> For they will be exempt and free
> From lovers' doubts and anxiety.
> No other gem than turquoise on her breast
> Can to the loving, doubting heart bring rest.

The primary quality of the turquoise as a modern

birthstone is that it brings prosperity to the wearer, and symbolizes success and good fortune:

> If cold December gave you birth,
> The month of snow and ice and mirth,
> Place on your hand a turquoise blue,
> Success will bless whate'er you do.

One having the turquoise as his natal stone is in a fortunate position financially, for they are relatively inexpensive. However, one objection is that they are not as delicate-looking in rings, necklaces and bracelets as some of the other gems; for that reason girls may find them undesirable. For a boy, however, a good stone in a heavy silver ring is ideal.

A purchaser must be aware of "doctored" stones, for inferior specimens can be artifically treated so that their color can be intensified; eventually such coloration is likely to fade and the stone reverts to its natural color. Imitations made of glass may fool a buyer, who within a short time will discover that his birth symbol has lost its warmth.

ZIRCON

The jewelers undoubtedly selected the alternate December natal stone because its brilliant fire and many color variations contrast sharply with the turquoise. Frederick Pough rightly calls it "the forgotten gem," because its colorless variety resembles the diamond and the world of jewelry has forgotten the beauty of the many other colors. Another reason is that the various names by which it has been known, including hyacinth and jacinth, have not been familiar.

The origin of the name is uncertain; it was adapted from the French *zircone* which may have come from the Arabic *zarquin* meaning "red" or "vermilion," or the Persian *zargus*, "gold-colored." Zircon is a mineral silicate found in igneous rocks, with a small amount of iron.

Its chief characteristic is the wide variety of colors: The more usual are brown, brownish-red, violet, red, and gray; the less usual are yellow, green, orange, and colorless. The red and reddish-brown forms are known as hyacinth and jacinth. The colorless or white variety approaches the appearance of diamonds and can be cut to resemble them. A fairly new color, called starlight, is blue. Though never found in nature, a beautiful blue shade which is much in demand can be obtained by heating the golden-brown or yellow varieties. This heat treatment, if continued, can also make the zircon colorless.

Because it is hard and can be cut to show a dazzling brilliance, the zircon has attained increased popularity. Stones of all colors can be manufactured synthetically.

The best natural zircon comes from Ceylon, Thailand, and Vietnam, where the processing to blue is most popular.

The Smithsonian collection includes two browns—an 118-carat stone from Ceylon and one of 106 carats from

Thailand—besides excellent examples of the red-brown, blue, and green varieties.

Under the names hyacinth and jacinth, the zircon was a favorite stone of the ancient Arabs. The pages of the *Arabian Nights* contain many lists of these stones hoarded by Oriental monarchs. It was also a sacred stone of the Assyrians. The Romans treasured the yellow stones, as did residents of Europe during the Middle Ages.

The zircon, of whatever color, has been said to possess a magic which would counteract evil spirits and influences. Since it could drive away plagues, it was popular during the fourteenth century as a safeguard against the Black Death. Medically, a zircon was both an antidote to poison and an aid to digestion. During the sixteenth century, insomniacs used it to induce sleep. Writers have also stated that it could cheer the heart and make one secure from thunder, as well as increasing the wearer's riches, honor, and wisdom.

CHAPTER 15

YOUR BIRTHSTONE AND YOU

Each natal stone assigned to a calendar month or to a sign of the zodiac has a legacy of legend and superstition surrounding it. These stories have existed from ancient times, and in a less unquestioned form have survived to the present time.

To many, these stories of splendor and riches, of good and bad luck, and of superhuman powers seem ridiculous. More or less sophisticated and educated modern individuals are often impatient with and intolerant of such beliefs. Yet they should be considered as an exhibition of the steps by which man, with his accumulation of knowledge, has progressed.

In reading these ancient legends and myths pertaining to one's birthstone, it is necessary to realize that scientific knowledge is quite recent compared with the vast time span in the history of man. A lack of proven fact therefore encouraged beliefs which to us are absurd. The mysteries of nature and the secrets of the mineral world and the mysteries beneath the earth's crust were difficult for the peoples of the past to understand.

Seers, prophets, and soothsayers misled the people, and the superstitious and gullible accepted their interpretations without question. In the Middle Ages, for example, the belief in evil spirits was common; therefore any assistance which would give the common man the power to overcome them would be readily welcomed. When knowledge of the human body was limited—the science of medicine did not begin to develop until the seventeenth and eighteenth centuries —it was quite natural that the powers and magic of gems and charms would be accepted as an aid to good health. Their influences over human life—good or bad luck, the future, love, fidelity, and the factors which contribute to one's happiness—were taken seriously.

The powers of birthstones, then, represent the thoughts of the past and are interesting if only on that basis. They need not be accepted. They can be laughed at, but these beliefs existed in certain periods of history, and they form the background for each particular natal stone.

Aside from the legacy of these beliefs, there is always the individual beauty of the stones. Each has its particular appeal. Taste and fashion play their parts, and many prefer to wear a precious or semiprecious stone which is not assigned to their birth date.

The lure of gems throughout the vast span of human history is a fact. Gems serve a purpose in enriching our lives, and their wearers can take pleasure in owning a small part of the wonderful, mysterious, often dazzling world of gemstones.

REFERENCES

The many full-length books on various individual gemstones are not included in this list.

Axon, Gordon V., *The Wonderful World of Gems*. New York, Criterion Books, 1967.

Baerwald, Marcus, and Tom Mahoney, *The Story of Jewelry*. New York, Abelard-Schuman, 1960.

Bauer, J. and A., and H. Jelinek, *A Book of Jewels*. Artia, 1966.

Curran, Mona, *A Treasury of Jewels and Gems*. New York, Emerson Books, 1967.

Desautels, Paul E., *Gems in the Smithsonian Institution*. Washington, Smithsonian Institution, 1965 (Publication No. 4608).

Fisher, P. J., *The Science of Gems*. New York, Scribner, 1966.

Hoyt, Edwin P., *The Jewel Hunters*. Boston, Atlantic-Little Brown, 1967.

Kozminsky, Isidore, *The Magic and Science of Jewels and Stones*. New York, Putnam, 1922.

Kraus, Edward H., and Chester B. Slawson, *Gems and Gem Materials*. 5th ed. New York, McGraw-Hill, 1947.

Kunz, George F., *The Curious Lore of Precious Stones*. Philadelphia, Lippincott, 1913.

———, *The Magic of Jewels and Charms*. Philadelphia, Lippincott, 1915.

Orpen, Adela E., *Stories About Famous Precious Stones*. New York, Lothrop, 1890.

Pearl, Richard M., *Wonders of Gems.* New York, Dodd, Mead, 1963.

Pough, Frederick H., *The Story of Gems and Semiprecious Stones.* Irvington-on-Hudson, New York, Harvey House, 1967.

Rogers, Frances, and Alice Beard, *5000 Years of Gems and Jewelry.* Rev. ed. Philadelphia, Lippincott, 1947.

Shelley, Frank, *Legends of Gems.* Broadway Publishing Co., 1905.

Shipley, Robert M., ed., *The Dictionary of Gems and Gemology.* 5th ed. Los Angeles, Gemological Institute of America, 1951.

Twining, Lord, *History of the Crown Jewels of Europe.* London, Batsford, 1960.

Weinstein, Michael, *The World of Jewel Stones.* New York, Sheridan House, 1958.

Wilson, Mab, *Gems.* New York, Viking, 1967.

Wodiska, Julius, *A Book of Precious Stones.* New York, Putnam, 1909.

Zim, Herbert S., and Paul K. Shaffer, *Rocks and Minerals: A Guide to Familiar Minerals, Gems, Ores and Rocks.* New York, Golden Press, 1957.

Additional valuable information may be obtained in issues of the following periodicals, among others, indexed in *Readers' Guide to Periodical Literature* under the headings Gems, Precious stones, and names of individual gems: *Hobbies, Jewelers Circular-Keystone, Lapidary Journal, Natural History, Nature Magazine.*

INDEX

Abercorn, Marquis of, 67
Abrasives, 29
Africa, 49, 112
Agate, 4, 6, 83; in birthstone lists, 13; in High Priest's breastplate, 18
Alexander, Crown Prince of Russia, 73
Alexandra, Empress of Russia, 92–93
Alexandrite, 73–75; color changes, 73–74; hardness, 5, 39, 74; in birthstone lists, 13; in zodiac list, 20, 64; synthetic, 14, 74
Alfonso XII, King of Spain, 103–4
Almandine garnet, 28
Aluminum, 14, 58, 90, 111, 115
Amber, 4; in High Priest's breastplate, 18
American Museum of Natural History, 79–80, 88, 93, 112, 113, 117
American National Retail Jewelers' Association: birthstone list, 13, 14–15, 21
Amethyst, 33–38; beliefs and superstitions, 24, 25, 36–37; characteristics assigned to, 22–23 (tables), 37–38; color, 9, 25, 33, 34, 36, 38; gem of royalty, 36; hardness, 5; in birthstone lists, 13; in High Priest's breastplate, 18; in zodiac list, 21, 33; myth, 33–34; religious use, 35–36
Amulet, 6, 44, 119
Andradite garnets, 28
April: birthstone for, 20, 47–56 (see also Diamond); in birth-
stone lists, 13; in zodiac, 20, 47, 57
Aquamarine, 39–42; beliefs and superstitions, 24, 41–42; characteristics assigned to, 42; color, 9, 39–40, 42; hardness, 5, 39, 40; in birthstone lists, 13; in High Priest's breastplate, 18; in zodiac list, 21, 39; museum specimens, 40–41; myth, 39
Aquarius: birthstone for, 21, 33–38 (see also Amethyst); in zodiac list, 21, 33
Arabian Nights, 54, 123
Arabian Sea, 90
Arabs, 37, 69–70, 100, 117–18, 123; birthstone list, 13
Aries: birthstone for, 20, 47–56 (see also Diamond); in zodiac list, 20, 47
Arizona, 88, 116
Artificial gems, see Synthetic gems
Assyria, 123
Asterism, 72
Astrology, 19–20, 21, 24–25; see also Zodiac
August: birthstones for, 20, 83–89 (see also Peridot; Sardonyx); in birthstone lists, 13; in zodiac, 20, 83
Augustus, Emperor of Rome, 86
Australia, 43, 49, 59, 77, 87, 91, 94, 98, 103, 115
Austria, 28, 59

Babylon, 44, 58
Bavaria, 28
Beads, 14, 29